The Black Dilemma
by John Herbers

Conflict and Compromise:
The Dynamics of American Foreign Policy
by Richard Halloran

Eastern Europe in the Soviet Shadow
by Harry Schwartz

Madman in a Lifeboat:
Issues of the Environmental Crisis
by Gladwin Hill

The USSR Today
by Harry A. Rositzke

𝕿𝖍𝖊 𝕹𝖊𝖜 𝖄𝖔𝖗𝖐 𝕿𝖎𝖒𝖊𝖘

SURVEY SERIES

THEODORE M. BERNSTEIN
GENERAL EDITOR

The New York Times Survey Series comprises books that deal comprehensively yet comprehensibly with subjects of wide interest, presenting the facts impartially and drawing conclusions honestly.

The series draws on the great information resources of *The New York Times* and on the talents, backgrounds, and insights of specially qualified authors, mostly members of the *Times* staff.

The subjects range from the relatively particular problems of civilized life to the broadest conceivable problems concerning whether civilized life, or any kind of life, will continue to be possible on this planet.

The hope is that the books will be essentially informative, perhaps argumentative, but beyond that stimulative to useful, constructive thinking by the citizens who ultimately must share in civilization's decisions.

Conflict
and Compromise

Conflict
and
Compromise

THE DYNAMICS
OF AMERICAN
FOREIGN POLICY

RICHARD HALLORAN

The John Day Company
An Intext Publisher
NEW YORK

Published in hardcover by
The John Day Company, 257 Park Avenue South, New York, N.Y. 10010

Published in softcover by
Intext Press, 257 Park Avenue South, New York, N.Y. 10010

Published on the same day in Canada by Longman Canada Limited.

Printed in the United States of America

Library of Congress Cataloging in Publication Data

Halloran, Richard, 1930-
    Conflict and compromise.

    (The New York times survey series)
    1. United States—Foreign relations—1969-
I. Title.
JX1417.H34   327.73   72–2269

ISBN: 0-381-98112-6 (hardcover)
            0-381-90002-9 (paperback)

For my Mother and Father

There is no textbook prescription for organizing the machinery of foreign policy and no procedural formula for making wise decisions.

—President Richard M. Nixon,
February 18, 1970, in a report
to the Congress on foreign policy

Contents

Preface

THIS VOLUME is a brief but broad survey of the people, institutions, and processes involved in making decisions on the foreign policy of the United States. It is intended for the general reader and for that all-important person, the average American citizen. It was written in the belief that Americans will continue to be vitally interested in their government's foreign policy and how it is made even as they increasingly turn their attention to the domestic problems of the 1970's. With the United States lessening its engagements abroad, the execution of foreign policy will require even more diplomatic skill on the part of the nation's political leaders and more critical perception and understanding on the part of American citizens.

That became particularly true after the summer of 1971, during which President Nixon boldly altered United States policy toward China and forced a fundamental change in the international economic system. All that flowed from those moves cracked apart the shaky but relatively stable international balance of power and sent the major powers searching for a new equilibrium in the world order. It was evident, as the President met with the leaders of America's allies in late 1971 and early 1972, and then went on his journeys to Peking and Moscow, that the uncertain situation would tax to the fullest the abilities of the nation's political leaders, all elements of the foreign policy apparatus, and the public before a new balance of power was achieved.

I should add that the book is not a research work with all of the accoutrements of a scholarly study. Where I have thought necessary, I have included the source of information in the text. The major portion, however, came from my own experience and from the files of my colleagues in the Washington Bureau of *The New York Times*. I should note that many of the examples that illustrate a decision have to do with American policy in Asia since that is the area with which I am most familiar. But that is only accidental and the description of the policy-making process applies to all areas of foreign affairs.

A word of genuine thanks is due to Theodore M. Bernstein, Editorial Director of The New York Times Book and Education Division, who conceived the idea for the book and patiently guided it to completion. In addition, several members of the foreign policy bureaucracy in Washington contributed ideas and information at various stages along the way, for which I am grateful. In the best bureaucratic tradition, they asked to remain anonymous. Even so, they and Mr. Bernstein must be absolved of the responsibility for the accuracy of facts and the pertinence of interpretations, for that is mine alone.

RICHARD HALLORAN

Bethesda, Maryland
January 1972

Conflict
and Compromise

1

The Adversary
Process

THE FIRST makers of American foreign policy were members of a Committee of Secret Correspondence set up by patriots just before the Revolution. They sent agents to Europe, particularly to France, to obtain arms, ammunition, and political support for the coming conflict with Great Britain. The Committee also dispatched agents to England to seek information on the sentiment there toward the Colonies. After 1776, the secrecy was dropped and the group became the Committee for Foreign Affairs. Its bureaucracy totaled one clerk, who served for $70 a month.

Americans were not much concerned with the outside world in those days or, indeed, in the decades that followed. President Washington's Farewell Address, in which he admonished his compatriots to avoid entangling alliances, set the tone of neutrality for almost 150 years. Consequently, the bureaucracy charged with the formulation and execution of foreign policy grew but slowly. Even by 1941, on the eve of World War II, the Department of State had only 1,200 officers in Washington and around the world. Few others in government were involved at all in foreign affairs. Dean Acheson, who came into the Department in 1941 and later became Secretary of State, has written that "for the most part the prewar

Department was concerned with treaties of commerce or navigation." He said that "the general run of business involved extricating Americans from trouble abroad or helping them engage in commercial ventures from which others wished to exclude them."

All of that has changed over the last thirty years as America has become the world's most powerful nation and has assumed international responsibilities with entangling alliances in every corner of the globe. The basic objectives of the nation's foreign policy today are two. The first is to preserve the nation's independence and national security by preventing other nations from doing harm to it. The second is to promote a multitude of national interests intended to better the lives of Americans, either by improving the international community in which all nations live or by obtaining for the United States a particular advantage. A mutual security treaty with an ally helps to provide for the military defense of the United States. An international agreement that bans the testing of nuclear weapons in the atmosphere cuts down on the radiation and pollution affecting all peoples. There is possibly a third objective that is altruistic. A foreign policy may be devised in enlightened self-interest and couched in terms that make it appear to the public to be altruistic. The Marshall Plan to reconstruct Europe after World War II and the many programs of economic aid since then are perhaps good examples. But in the world of realpolitik, even those polices are at heart intended to preserve the national security or to enhance the national interests.

To cope with those many-faceted responsibilities, what is known as the foreign policy community in Washington has ballooned in size and scope. All three branches of government are involved and there is hardly a department or agency in Washington that is not somehow concerned on an almost daily basis with one aspect of foreign policy or another. At the center of the vast and unwieldy apparatus of foreign policy is the President and the staff of the National Security Council in the White House. The Department of State, the Department of Defense, and the Central Intelligence Agency are within the inner circle. More than a dozen other departments are ranged around the perimeter within the executive branch. But there are other seats of power, most notably in the Congress, that have constitutional, political, and economic roles to play in foreign policy. The judiciary, as the enforcer of the law and the ruler on legal precedent, has a usually peripheral but occasionally decisive say in foreign affairs. Lobbyists for labor, industry, and other vested interests have influence often unseen and underrated. Beyond the apparatus is the public, which can have some say on immediate decisions and has everything to say on the long-term trends.

Decisions in foreign policy, like so much else in the governing of the United States, are made through the adversary process. A particular policy is the result of a compromise that comes out of conflict. There are conflicts between internationalist and isolationist ideologies, between foreign and domestic interests, among the branches of government, among the departments within the executive branch, between the civilian and military sectors, among political and bureaucratic personalities, between idealism and expedience. Most of the resulting compromises are invisible, with perhaps only 5 to 10 percent ever reaching the public eye. On issues of less than critical importance, and these are by far the majority, decisions are made at the middle level of the bureaucracy, whether within one department or among representatives of several agencies. The practice of bureaucracy dictates that every official remotely concerned with the question at hand must be consulted and his concurrence obtained. If one does not agree, he either kills the proposal, or it goes ahead with his objections noted, or, more likely, the issue is passed up to the next level for resolution. Similarly, more serious questions are debated at the sub-cabinet and cabinet level and each department involved must concur. On the critical issues, or on those that cannot be decided below, the President is the final arbiter within the executive branch. It is those decisions that make the headlines.

Because the process is complicated and time-consuming, some participants have tried to accord it a mystique, the understanding of which is given only to a chosen few. But the process is more hidden than mysterious. Politicians prefer to maneuver behind the scenes until it is to their political advantage to bring a decision into the open. Bureaucrats infighting with other bureaucrats over the content of a policy recommendation want to do so outside the scrutiny of their superiors or the public. One department bargaining with another fears that disclosure of its position would weaken its hand or prove embarrassing if the final decision goes against it. American diplomats negotiating with foreign diplomats want to maintain secrecy to preserve maximum advantage. Throughout the process, everyone wants to tuck away mistakes and to clothe politically unpalatable policies in the most hopeful rhetoric that can be conjured up. But the making of decisions in foreign policy need not be a mystery. The organization of people and departments and machinery was devised by human beings and therefore can be understood by other human beings. Into each decision goes the same mix of ambition, prejudice, information—and misinformation—dedication, and emotion as into decisions made elsewhere. If the Secretary of State has a fight with his wife one morning, it can affect his day just like anybody else's.

Two particular characteristics of American foreign policy should be noted. One is the impact of internal pressures on external policies. Many of the decisions on Indochina made by Presidents Johnson and Nixon were governed by domestic political pressures, primarily dissent. The policy of the United States in the Middle East has been strongly influenced by the relatively small but highly articulate Jewish vote to favor Israel. The correct but cool attitude of the United States toward South Africa, which practices strict racial segregation, has been a response to the political realities of the racial issue within America.

The second is the atmosphere of crisis in which many decisions are made. Because the decisions are often complicated, because no decision will ever satisfy everyone, because the process is cumbersome, decisions are often postponed until they absolutely have to be made. Administration after administration has come to office with the promise that it will plan foreign policy in a way to preclude crises. But once in office, the administration has been forced by the onrush of events to improvise and to patch together a policy in a hurry to meet an unforeseen need.

In the making of a foreign policy decision, whether in an emergency or in a routine fashion, meetings are the essence of life in the Washington bureaucracy. To thrash out recommendations, advocates and adversaries meet to discuss, debate, and, hopefully, to decide. Each brings to a meeting a different point of view based on his own interests, perceptions, and knowledge. The diplomat for the State Department is concerned with foreign political implications; the military officer from the Department of Defense looks to military consequences; the White House staffer thinks of the domestic political posture of the President.

A capable bureaucrat in a meeting is something of a guided missile. He is programmed first by his own grasp of the issue that comes from years of studying the intricacies of it. He is directed by the thinking of his office or his department, the political pressures of which he is aware, and the personal contacts he has built up throughout the bureaucracy. An advocate with a strong personality, the ability to marshal arguments, and a persuasive presentation based on thorough homework can carry a decision over those less able or less well prepared. It matters little whether the department he represents has primary responsibility for the problem at hand. The representative of a department only marginally concerned can come out on top of the bureaucrat from a department deeply involved if he knows what he is doing.

Similarly, a capable bureaucrat can influence policy at levels well above his own by coming up with a knowledgeable, persuasive argument. Skilled middle-level officials regularly use their superiors as amplifiers to make their views known, albeit without having the source identified. When the senior man is either uninterested or too busy to give the particular issue his full attention, the junior official can overwhelm him with fact and analysis and leave him almost helpless to do anything but agree to the junior's recommendation.

Another essential element in the decision-making process is what are called "papers" in Washington. Easily the best known collection of those in modern American history is the Pentagon Papers published by *The New York Times* in 1971. Beyond their political, diplomatic, and military significance, the Pentagon Papers are a fascinating study of the role of men, meetings, and papers in a period of more than twenty years of policy decisions on Indochina. The papers range from full-scale reports to short personal notes, from cables between Washington and Saigon to minutes of meetings, from intelligence estimates to instructions from the President—in short, the entire gamut of Washington papers. As illustrated by the Pentagon Papers, a Washington policy paper can run from one to a hundred typewritten pages, setting out a problem, the facts and analyses that bear on it, and one or more proposals for solving it. Recommendations go up in papers to those in authority for decision. Instructions come down in papers to those who must carry out the policy.

Much fun is made of papers in Washington because they epitomize the red tape of bureaucracy, but the system clearly could not function without them. The question is not whether things should be committed to writing but whether what is written down is worthwhile. Much is, but some is not. Papers are further intended to focus discussion on pertinent points. Meetings tend to ramble at best and without a paper to which advocates and adversaries can address themselves, little would ever get done. In government, as elsewhere, writing forces people to think a question through.

Having a decision on paper is also intended, though not always successfully, to prevent a misunderstanding of a decision or a policy. A decision on paper helps to insure that all who need to know the decision are informed, and informed in the manner intended by the decision-makers and not as someone else interpreted it. While subordinates can put different interpretations on a policy decision, they are less likely to distort it if it is on paper rather than passed down by word of mouth. If a policy is to be changed, papers give the decision-makers a point of departure from which to start the shift. Papers also give continuity to policy in a government where people come and go and where administrations change.

This is not to say that everything in Washington is written down. Much is not, either in the recommendation or implementation stages. Washington is a buzzing grapevine of seemingly trivial but often vital talk that goes on at lunches, receptions, and dinners. But many political leaders and bureaucrats are critical of the misunderstandings that arise and the mistakes that are made when things are not written down. That was particularly true during the administration of President Johnson, a secretive man who disliked having things recorded and thus possibly limiting his options later.

Still another essential element in the policy-making process is the public pronouncement. Speeches, press releases, news conferences, and intentional "leaks" to the press are an integral part of making decisions on foreign policy. The address of a cabinet officer before a ladies' club in Dubuque may appear to be a public service or an effort to explain policy to get support for it. There is some of that, but more often the speech is intended to build political pressure by one department that is in a dispute with another. Leaks to the press are a favorite device for that. Similarly, the answer to a question given by the President or the Secretary of State in a news conference may appear to be satisfying the curiosity of the reporter and, hopefully, enlightening the public. But the remarks, carefully prepared and couched in terms loaded with nuance, are frequently directed at an ally or an adversary abroad. The United States can thus communicate with foreign governments without seeming to have put an official stamp on the message.

There are occasions, too, when a major speech by the President or another senior member of the administration is in reality a message to warring factions in the bureaucracy that a political decision has been made. So long as a decision has not been made public, many politicians and bureaucrats feel that it is not final and that they may continue to argue the issue. But once it is made

9

public, the decision seems to be set in concrete. That serves both to stop the infighting and to set before the nation the policy of government. There seems to be something in the American psyche that makes a public statement a commitment and a reality. President Woodrow Wilson once proclaimed the doctrine of "open convenants, openly arrived at." Few covenants are openly arrived at, either within the United States government or between the United States and another nation. The practicalities of bureaucratic or diplomatic bargaining preclude that idealistic manner of reaching agreements. On the other hand, a secret agreement appears to have little standing in the American way of thinking and it is not really an agreement or a decision until it is put out where citizens can see it.

2

The Center of Power

THE PRESIDENT of the United States is clearly the single most powerful person in the making of American foreign policy. He is the chief executive officer of government, with all of its resources at his command. He is the commander-in-chief of the armed forces, with the authority to deploy them for national security. He has the power to propose treaties and to enter into executive agreements with other nations. His Office of Management and Budget, formerly the Bureau of the Budget, controls the flow of funds into the executive departments that formulate and execute his foreign policy. Beyond his constitutional and statutory powers, the President has the substantial political power that has gravitated to the White House since World War II. But no two Presidents have employed their powers in the same way. Each has brought to his administration a distinctive style and approach to the making of decisions in foreign policy. Moreover, the President lacks absolute power and is subject to constraints, especially from the Congress, in his every move. In the conflict of making foreign policy, he is the Ultimate Compromiser.

During World War II, President Roosevelt slapped together a military and diplomatic apparatus to meet the urgent needs of the nation. When it became apparent after the war that this would not be enough to meet the immense international responsibilities of the United States, President Truman proposed and the Congress enacted the National Security Act of 1947. It was intended to bring some order to foreign policy and is still the foundation on which any administration builds its machinery for handling foreign affairs.

The centerpiece of the act was the establishment of the National Security Council (NSC). It was "to advise the President with respect to the integration of domestic, foreign, and military policies relating to the national security so as to enable the military services and other departments and agencies to cooperate more effectively in matters involving the national security." The NSC was to be chaired by the President, with the other members being the Vice President, the Secretary of State, the Secretary of Defense, and the Director of the Office of Emergency Preparedness. The Director of Central Intelligence and the Chairman of the Joint Chiefs of Staff were named advisers.

From the beginning, each President has used the NSC in a markedly different manner. President Truman saw the council as the highest and final tribunal for hearing recommendations on policy before he made the decision. His Secretary of State, Dean Acheson, said in his book, *Present at the Creation*, that "for centuries, courts have required all parties in interest to be present before the court at the same time with the right to be heard and to hear one another. President Truman introduced this procedure into executive administration. To it he added an equally ancient, and in administration equally novel, practice of law: the decision was immediately reduced to writing."

"The vehicle for these innovations," Mr. Acheson continued, "was the National Security Council. . . . It was kept small; aides and brief-carriers were excluded, a practice . . . that made free and frank debate possible. Those present came prepared to present their views themselves, and had previously filed memoranda. Matters brought before the Council were of importance worthy of the

12

personal attention of the highest officers and decision by the President."

Under President Eisenhower, the functioning of the NSC changed. General Eisenhower preferred to stay clear of details and wanted decisions worked out at lower levels. They were to rise to the top for final approval at regular weekly meetings of the NSC. Mr. Eisenhower introduced the concept that the NSC take into account the government's budget in its deliberations and once wrote that "the responsibilities of the NSC as an advisory body were broadened to recognize the relationship between military and economic strength."

To obtain the "agreed recommendations" that he desired, President Eisenhower added several subordinate committees to the NSC. They, in turn, evolved an elaborate process for preparing policy papers on everything that might come before the NSC. Critics of the Eisenhower Administration contended that the NSC apparatus was unwieldy and produced policy studies that were too general to give precise guidance to those officials who were responsible for carrying them out.

In contrast to President Eisenhower's studied approach was the free-wheeling style of President Kennedy. He cared little for set procedures or established bureaucratic machinery and relied primarily on the judgment of men he trusted, no matter where they sat in—or out of—government. He abolished or ignored large parts of the NSC apparatus and abandoned the practice of collective decisions. Theodore Sorensen, the President's close adviser, said in his book, *Kennedy*, that the President "relied instead on informal meetings and direct contacts—on a personal White House staff, the Budget Bureau and ad hoc task forces to probe and define issues for his decision—on special Presidential emissaries and constant Presidential phone calls and memoranda—on placing Kennedy men in each strategic spot. Particularly in 1961 and particularly on national security matters, he talked at the White House or by telephone to lower-level officers and experts with first-hand knowledge or responsibility."

President Kennedy made the position of Assistant to the President for National Security Affairs, which had been set up by President Eisenhower, into an office of considerable influence. Mr. Kennedy chose McGeorge Bundy, of Harvard, as his assistant to head the NSC staff, which became intimately involved in the decision-making process. But President Kennedy deemphasized the NSC itself. He called more meetings during a crisis than at other times to get the views of responsible officers on the record and to give the political appearance that his administration was moving with dispatch. But the actual decisions were made by the President outside of the NSC. During the Cuban missile crisis in 1962, for instance, the President turned to a small group of personal advisers, some inside and others outside the government, and to the NSC only after the decisions were made.

President Johnson's methods for making decisions somewhat resembled those of President Kennedy but he had neither the interest nor the range in foreign affairs of his predecessor. Mr. Johnson delved deeply into specific problems, most notably Vietnam, but only because his office demanded it of him. He required immense amounts of information and recommendations from a variety of sources inside and outside of government. But he had little use for formal machinery and left things much as he had inherited them from Mr. Kennedy.

President Johnson's major forum for the discussion of foreign policy was his regular Tuesday luncheon meeting with Secretary of State Dean Rusk, Secretary of Defense Robert S. McNamara, and Assistant to the President McGeorge Bundy and later Walt W. Rostow. Occasionally others were invited but mainly it was that group, working sometimes from an agenda and other times without, that gave the President advice on the highest level. Mr. Johnson also relied heavily on the personal advice given him by his closest confidants outside the government.

Beyond that, President Johnson was on the telephone a dozen times a day or had officials into his office as he worked his way toward a decision. He wanted all possible alternatives brought before him before he decided. He tried to preclude having anyone foreclose a decision by revealing little of his own thinking until he was ready. Mr. Johnson preferred to delay a decision until the last possible moment on the theory that late information or ideas would be useful. The phrase "keeping the options open" became a byword in Washington during the Johnson Administration.

When President Nixon took office in January, 1969, he instituted a decision-making process that reflected his own approach but drew something from each of his four immediate predecessors. Mr. Nixon, a deliberate man trained in the law, wanted an orderly system that relied upon written proposals and decisions. He put together a large apparatus but insisted on clear lines of communication. The system provided for task forces but as an integral part of the machinery. Mr. Nixon required that all alternatives be brought before him but in a methodical and impersonal manner. He preferred to make his decision alone and became known for his lined, yellow, legal pads on which he scribbled his thoughts while by himself.

Shortly after Mr. Nixon's inauguration, the White House announced that the NSC would be the principal forum for the consideration of foreign policy issues requiring Presidential decision. The President designated his Secretary of State, William P. Rogers, as his senior adviser on foreign policy and assigned to the Department of State the authority for directing and coordinating the overseas activities of all government departments except for military commands that reported to the Pentagon. Within a short time, however, it became clear that the President's principal adviser on foreign policy was his Assistant for National Security Affairs, Dr. Henry A. Kissinger. After three years in office, it became apparent that Dr. Kissinger was the President's only major adviser on critical issues, particularly the bold diplomatic moves made toward China. Secretary Rogers and the Department of State were relegated to a secondary role of coordinating policy studies and executing decisions.

Dr. Kissinger, who had been born in Germany, was a scholar

who specialized in geopolitical strategy at Harvard before joining the Nixon Administration. He was largely responsible for designing the highly-centralized NSC system that Mr. Nixon wanted. Moreover, Dr. Kissinger had his hands on the valves that controlled the flow in the decision-making process, particularly in determining what should receive Presidential attention and what need not. He was chairman of several important committees within the system, a member of others, and was responsible for the preparation of studies and agenda for NSC meetings. On a personal level, Dr. Kissinger had frequent access to President Nixon and usually traveled with him on Presidential getaways to Camp David, Key Biscayne, and San Clemente. Dr. Kissinger's influence derived from his intense, driving personality, his perceptive grasp of the issues, a view of international politics that was fundamentally the same as the President's, and the evolution of his office. President Nixon and Dr. Kissinger made it among the most influential in Washington.

When he revitalized the NSC, President Nixon ordered that several subordinate groups be set up to assist the NSC in its deliberations and to see that his decisions were carried out. At the base of the pyramid were six Interdepartmental Groups, each headed by an Assistant Secretary of State in charge of a geographic region. Other members came from the NSC staff, the Defense Department, the CIA, and the staff of the JCS. Representatives from other agencies were brought in when issues pertaining to their agencies were involved. The Groups' basic responsibilities were to prepare policy papers for consideration by the NSC. Those papers included the background and specific issues on a particular problem and a list of alternative solutions, with the pros and cons of each noted and the proponents and opponents of each listed.

NSC Ad Hoc Groups were set up on about the same level with the Interdepartmental Groups. They dealt with questions that cut across regional boundaries, such as arms control, and with pressing problems such as Vietnam. Their membership comprised representatives from all agencies concerned with the question at hand.

At the next level up were four groups: The NSC Senior Review Group, the Defense Program Review Committee, the Washington Special Action Group, and the Undersecretaries Committee. Dr. Kissinger was chairman of the first three and a member of the fourth. Senior officials from State, Defense, and CIA also sat on most of the committees, giving the system cohesion and underscoring its centralized nature.

The Senior Review Group was charged with reviewing policy papers prepared by the Interdepartmental Groups to decide whether the issue was important enough to warrant consideration by the NSC and the President, to determine whether all of the pertinent facts, cost estimates, and differing agency viewpoints had been included, and to see whether the paper contained all of the realistic alternatives for solutions. The Senior Review Group did the same for papers coming from the Ad Hoc Groups and those coming from one department if it alone had been assigned a task.

The Defense Program Review Committee was somewhat larger than the others. Besides Dr. Kissinger, the members were the Undersecretary of State, the Deputy Secretary of Defense, the Chairman of the JCS, the Director of Central Intelligence, the Director of the Office of Management and Budget, and the Chairman of the President's Council of Economic Advisers. In addition, the Director of the Arms Control and Disarmament Agency, the President's Science Adviser, and the Chairman of the Atomic Energy Commission participated when questions under their purview came up. The Committee was responsible for measuring major defense programs, which require tremendous sums of money, against other needs in foreign and domestic policy. Among its continuing tasks was to plan defense budgets years into the future so that the President and the NSC had a projection of what might be coming. The five-year forecast was revised each year.

The Washington Special Action Group was originally set up in 1969 to handle a potential crisis after North Korean aircraft shot down an American reconnaissance plane over the Sea of Japan. But it was made a permanent part of the system and was responsible for spotting potential crises and preparing integrated diplomatic and military contingency plans for handling them. The group was also called on to advise the President in crises that had not been anticipated, such as the decision to send troops into Cambodia in 1970. In addition to Dr. Kissinger, the members were the Director of Central Intelligence, the Chairman of the JCS, the Deputy Secretary of Defense, and the Undersecretary of State for Political Affairs.

The same men were members of the Undersecretaries Committee, except that the Undersecretary of State was chairman. While Elliot L. Richardson was Undersecretary in the first year of the Nixon Administration, the committee had some influence, largely because Mr. Richardson was a capable political administrator. When he was named Secretary of Health, Education, and Welfare, there was a long hiatus before his successor was designated and the committee lost momentum. It was intended to be primarily operational, overseeing the execution of policy. It also was responsible for resolving disagreements that did not require NSC consideration.

The NSC system appeared to have been neatly organized, but it was fluid in action. Few decisions followed the same track as they coursed through the process. How each was handled depended on the nature of the question, the urgency with which it had to be decided, the quality of staff work, and the attention given it by Dr. Kissinger. Much depended, too, on President Nixon's personal interest. He involved himself in some issues at an early stage and followed it through the entire process. On others, he permitted the system to function almost according to its theoretical conception, reserving to himself the final, critical decision before the policy went into effect.

A nearly classic case of routine functioning was the decision to return the island of Okinawa to Japan. Okinawa, lying in the Ryukyu Islands southwest of Japan, was captured by the United States during the closing days of World War II. Over the years, the United States built a vast complex of military bases there to support operations around the Asian littoral from Korea to Singapore. But the United States never laid territorial claim to the island. The policy of all administrations was that Okinawa would be returned to Japan when the security situation in East Asia permitted.

In the late 1960's, however, the rise of an intense Japanese nationalism generated strong demands for the reversion of the island to Japanese political control. By the time Mr. Nixon came to office, it was apparent that vital American political, economic, and military relationships with Japan would be severely damaged unless a date for reversion was set.

In late January, 1969, Dr. Kissinger sent a three-line memorandum to Secretary of State Rogers asking for a thorough study of all aspects of American relations with Japan, with the focus on Okinawa. The Secretary referred the memo to Marshall Green, the Assistant Secretary for East Asian and Pacific Affairs and chairman of the Interdepartmental Group on East Asia. Mr. Green, in turn, organized a working group headed by the officer in charge of Japanese affairs in the State Department. The Defense Department had three representatives: one from the Office of International Security Affairs, the diplomatic arm of the Secretary of Defense; a second from the JCS to bring the military point of view; and a third from the Department of the Army, which was responsible for the administration of the island. An official from the Treasury was included because reversion would entail questions of shifting from dollar to yen currency and would affect the United States balance of payments. The Commerce Department represented American business enterprises that had investments in Okinawa. The United States Information Agency official brought his organization's views on the powerful Voice of America transmitting station on Okinawa. A man from the CIA dealt with the fate of the agency's support base for operations throughout Asia. Finally, a representative from the NSC staff made known the views of the President and Dr. Kissinger.

During meetings through the winter of 1969, the working group wrote a fifty-page paper known as a National Security Study

Memorandum, or NSSM. The chairman did most of the drafting, circulating copies to his colleagues for their advice, refinements, and consent. Within the overall context of American relations with Japan, the working group posed several alternatives for solving the Okinawa question that ranged from leaving the status of the island as it was to giving it back to Japan and withdrawing all American military forces. Most attention was centered on options that would return Okinawa to Japan without seriously eroding the capability of the United States to use the bases there to fulfill its commitments elsewhere in Asia.

The major disagreement was quickly identified—how could Okinawa be returned without the United States giving up the right to deploy nuclear weapons there? The Japanese government, sensitive to the "nuclear allergy" of the Japanese people that resulted from the atomic bombings of Hiroshima and Nagasaki in 1945, had demanded an agreement that included the withdrawal of nuclear weapons. Within the working group, the representatives of the State Department and the Office of International Security Affairs at Defense contended that the United States must agree to take the weapons out. Otherwise, political pressures in Japan would disrupt chances of reaching an agreement and thus would endanger the American alliance with Japan. The military officer from the JCS, however, argued that a withdrawal of nuclear weapons would seriously impair the American deterrent in the Western Pacific. He maintained that the United States could not fulfill its military commitments to Asian nations, including Japan, if Okinawa could not be used to store and launch nuclear weapons.

Both points of view were expressed in the NSSM that went through the Interdepartmental Group to the NSC Senior Review Group in late April. The Review Group, working mostly from a four-page summary of the overall United States-Japan relationship, focused its discussion on the Okinawa issue and particularly on the question of nuclear arms. The Group made few changes in the Interdepartmental Group's paper but could not resolve the nuclear issue. The opposing stands remained in the paper when it went to the NSC itself at the end of April. There, the Secretary of State and the Chairman of the JCS continued to disagree and debated the issue in the presence of the President. Mr. Nixon resolved the question by reserving to himself the final decision. He said that he would decide whether the United States would concede that point to Japan after all other points were negotiated with the Japanese government.

In late May, Dr. Kissinger prepared a page-and-a-half National Security Decision Memorandum, or NSDM, setting out the President's decision formally. Mr. Nixon had decided that the United States would begin negotiations with Japan and that Okinawa would be returned to Japan in 1972, provided certain conditions were met. The Japanese must agree to allow the United States to continue using the bases on Okinawa for conventional military operations with only slight restrictions. Japan must agree to American terms on settling a multitude of administrative and financial matters. And the Japanese would have to agree to easing the restrictions on American use of bases in Japan proper. The NSDM further directed the Undersecretaries Committee to prepare a strategy paper to guide American diplomats in their negotiations with the Japanese.

That paper outlined the objectives and phases of the negotiation, determined American strong points, assessed the Japanese negotiating position, specified points on which the United States would concede, and estimated areas in which Japanese concessions could be expected. The committee drafted instructions to the American ambassador in Tokyo to follow in negotiations with the Foreign Ministry in Tokyo. Once that was done, in July, the NSC system was largely finished with the Okinawa question. The Undersecretaries Committee monitored reports on the negotiations to see that American diplomats stayed on course but otherwise had little to do with the conversations.

Through the summer, Secretary of State Rogers met with Foreign Minister Kiichi Aichi of Japan several times in Washington and Tokyo to discuss the progress of the negotiations. In Tokyo, a special representative of the American government and the head of the American Bureau in the Foreign Ministry did most of the intensive negotiating until late October. By the time Prime Minister Eisaku Sato came to Washington in November, almost every question had been settled except the issue of nuclear withdrawal. Just before Mr. Sato arrived, President Nixon reviewed the results of the negotiations. He was satisfied and in his meeting with Mr. Sato agreed to the withdrawal of the nuclear weapons. The agreement in principle was announced in a joint communiqué at the conclusion of the Prime Minister's visit. Subsequent negotiations between American and Japanese diplomats brought agreement on the details, a treaty was adopted by the United States Senate and the Japanese Diet (Parliament), and in January, 1972, President Nixon and Prime Minister Sato agreed during a meeting at the Western White House in San Clemente, California, that reversion would take place on May 15, 1972.

3

Foggy Bottom

STANDING in the Foggy Bottom section of Washington, near the banks of the Potomac River, is an undistinguished concrete building that someone once said looked more like a federal penitentiary than the home of the United States Department of State. But there, along the south side of the seventh floor, is the paneled, carpeted, and hushed office of the Secretary of State, the senior member of the President's cabinet and, in theory, the President's chief adviser on foreign policy. The Secretary and the diplomats nestled in the warren of slightly dreary offices below are supposedly the principal figures among those who make or influence decisions in foreign policy. By and large, they are an able group of men and women, well-educated, impeccably mannered, knowledgeable in the languages and customs and politics and economics of more than a hundred nations, perceptive about the complicated forces at work in the world today, skilled in the arts of persuasion and negotiation, and dedicated to the service of their country.

Yet the department in which they serve is no longer preeminent in the making of foreign policy. Influence has, on the one hand, become centralized in the National Security Council staff in the White House. On the other hand, it has flowed away from the State Department to the Department of Defense, the Agency for International Development, the United States Information Agency, the Central Intelligence Agency, and to the "Little State Departments" that dot almost every other department and agency in Washington. The State Department has become less an initiator of ideas and policy and more a coordinator of initiatives from other agencies, plus being the channel of everyday negotiation and communication with other nations. Added to the shift in the locus of influence has been a paralysis within the department itself. It has failed to adapt to the diplomatic and bureaucratic needs that have emerged since World War II.

In 1970, senior and junior officials in the department began to recognize their loss of influence and to study ways to revitalize their role in making foreign policy. A major internal review produced this devastating self-criticism:

> The intellectual atrophy of the Department during the Fifties was a compound of presidential dissatisfaction, political reaction, Departmental conservatism, bureaucratic proliferation, and the inability or unwillingness of individual Secretaries of State to lead and stimulate the organization. Its creative arteries hardening, the Department as an institution was unable to meet adequately, and in some cases even to recognize, the innovative demands of the early Sixties. New ideas to cope with the Sino-Soviet dispute and the end of monolithic communism, the fast-emerging nuclear power balance, the growing disparity between rich nations and poor, and the diplomatic challenges of unconventional warfare, to name but a few of the rising problems, were not well received by an organization fearful of change.

> The leadership gap was crucial. Most Secretaries of State during the period, while often powerful and creative men in their own right, failed to use the Department to the full. Unschooled in modern management techniques, and harassed by enormous work pressures, most leading Departmental officers had not the time, inclination, or capacity to reach down into the ranks for new ideas, develop them, and then push them forcefully into the highest councils.

The mission of the State Department in any administration depends, first, on the authority given the Secretary of State by the President and, second, on the ability of the department to come up with the ideas and recommendations that serve his needs and to execute the policies that he sets. In recent years, that authority has gradually been diluted. President Truman's Secretaries of State, General George C. Marshall and Dean Acheson, both men of strong personality and extensive experience, were clearly his principal advisers on foreign policy. President Eisenhower turned over to his Secretary of State, John Foster Dulles, almost total responsibility for the conduct of foreign affairs.

But under President Kennedy a shift began. From the accounts of his biographers, it appears that Mr. Kennedy did not have full confidence in Secretary of State Dean Rusk and thought the State Department, which he referred to as a "bowl of jelly," was unresponsive to his wishes. President Johnson thought highly of Mr. Rusk, who stayed on as Secretary after President Kennedy's death, but he also consulted a number of other advisers. Mr. Johnson appeared, further, to have an instinctive distrust of officials in the department, many of whom he considered intellectual snobs. The influence of the department dropped even lower under President Nixon, who appointed a long-time personal and political friend, William P. Rogers, as Secretary of State. Mr. Rogers, unlike his predecessors, had not spent his adult life involved with foreign affairs and lacked experience and detailed knowledge of international relations. In sharp contrast, President Nixon's Assistant for National Security Affairs, Dr. Kissinger, had spent most of his career thinking and writing about foreign policy, which helped explain the flow of influence from the State Department to the National Security Council staff that he headed. That staff, paradoxically, included a large number of State Department officials.

The influence of the Department of State also depends on the leadership it is given by the Secretary and his ability to manage and use its resources, which are mostly the brains of its officials. There has been a steady decline in that capacity since the time of Secretary Marshall. General Marshall, after a lifetime in the army, was an effective manager who knew how to pull the best out of his staff. He instituted a Policy Planning Staff and drew from it many of the bold ideas needed to respond to the challenges of the late Forties.

His successor, Dean Acheson, was a brilliant lawyer who was skilled in dealing with men and issues but was less capable of managing a large organization. John Foster Dulles, who was President Eisenhower's Secretary of State, was even less interested in the administration of the department and put his full attention onto the critical issues of the day. Dean Rusk was interested in the performance of the department but had neither the time nor the inclination to stimulate imaginative thought because he was so deeply immersed in the problems of Vietnam. Mr. Rogers, like Mr. Acheson and Mr. Dulles, was a lawyer by training and unversed in effective management. A quiet, reserved man, Mr. Rogers lacked the personal dynamism to stir the department into action.

Beyond the personal relationships of the Secretaries of State with their Presidents and their own capacities for leadership were the sea changes that had taken place in the foreign policy community since the end of World War II. The United States came to rely on military power as a basic instrument of foreign policy, forging a web of alliances with more than forty nations that became a basis for America's political and economic relations with them. That gave the Department of Defense and the military services a major voice in foreign policy. The increasing complexity of foreign affairs led to the formation of new agencies that specialized in duties that were once those of the State Department. The Central Intelligence Agency in 1947, and later other agencies, took over much of the task of acquiring, collating, and interpreting the information on which decisions are based. The Agency for International Development and its predecessors dispensed economic aid, an instrument of foreign policy that always has some degree of political and diplomatic content. The United States Information Agency broadcast or published the propaganda intended to persuade other peoples to accept the United States' point of view. The Arms Control and Disarmament Agency undertook the tedious but vital task of trying to slow down the seemingly unending arms race. The Peace Corps went forth to give credibility to the good intentions of America in the developing nations. All were supposed to accept policy guidance from the Secretary of State but they operated, in effect, with almost complete autonomy.

Further, many of the domestically-oriented executive departments and agencies set up international bureaus to advance the cause, for example, of an American industry in trade or to protect American interests in international finance. Those bureaus often took a highly technical and parochial view of their responsibilities but they were influential because they did not have to weigh a myriad of conflicting interests and were able to pursue a course toward one objective. The officials who did the bargaining within the governmental adversary process had powerful political pressures behind them and were usually adept at using them in putting their views across. In contrast, officials from the State Department had to look for ways to compromise conflicting interests so that what they considered to be wider American interests were not damaged. They usually lacked political and public support and sometimes were accused of placing the interests of another nation before those of the United States. Moreover, many American diplomats were schooled in the niceties and rituals of international negotiation and were not equally adept at the bureaucratic infighting of Washington, which takes another form and has its own dynamics. Some, however, were good at both.

There have been a number of efforts within and without the State Department in recent years to revitalize it and to redefine its role in the foreign policy community. The latest was undertaken in 1970 by the Deputy Undersecretary of State for Administration, William B. Macomber. He outlined the objectives of the effort in a speech in early 1970, then organized thirteen task forces within the department to find ways in which the department could more forcefully make its influence felt. Out of that came a 610-page report in November, 1970, entitled "Diplomacy for the 70's: A Program of Management Reform for the Department of State." The authors of the report candidly recognized that "foreign relations were no longer the virtual monopoly of the Department of State and the issues of foreign policy were no longer exclusively diplomatic problems in the old and narrow sense." They recognized that the fundamental reasons for that were the proliferation of American activity abroad and the failure of the department to exert the leadership and the management of foreign policy. The report included about five hundred recommendations, some of them sweeping, others minute, intended to put the department in a posture to recapture a predominant position. They included suggestions for improving creativity and opening up lines of communication within the department and between the department and the rest of the executive branch, the Congress, and the public. Another set of recommendations focused on management, allocation of resources, planning, and staff work. A third group outlined possible improvements in the department's personnel practices. It remained to be seen, however, whether enough of the recommendations would be put into practice to permit the department to regain its stature. In the months immediately following the publication of the report, several changes were made in personnel practices. But they led only to the improved or more equitable treatment of Foreign Service officers and did little to attack the central issue of the department's leadership capabilities.

Despite its loss of influence, the State Department is still the major agency of the United States government that handles the day-to-day relations between America and other nations. Further, the department has considerable influence in the areas of the world and on the problems that receive less attention from the White House, the Defense Department, and the other organizations in the foreign policy community. And it still has channels into the major decision centers through the Secretary, who sits in the National Security Council, the Undersecretary, who is a member of several of the NSC subordinate committees, the Assistant Secretaries, who chair the Interdepartmental Groups, and other officials who are in daily contact with other key departments.

The top level of the department's organization comprises the Secretary, the Undersecretary, the Undersecretary for Political Affairs, who is the senior career diplomat, the Deputy Undersecretary for Economic Affairs, and the Deputy Undersecretary for Administration. Advising them are several staffs, including a planning staff that tries to look ahead, a press relations officer who acts as spokesman for the Secretary and the department, and a protocol staff that makes arrangements for visiting foreign dignitaries.

At what is known in Washington as the "working level" are six geographic bureaus and seven staff bureaus, each headed by an Assistant Secretary. Those officials are the workhorses of the department and are to it what a division or regional manager would be to a large corporation. The Assistant Secretaries take policy directives from the Secretary or the White House and put them into action. They take policy recommendations from officials in their bureaus and try to persuade the Secretary and the White House to accept them. On many questions, the Assistant Secretaries have the authority to make decisions and to issue instructions without referring to a higher officer, depending on the competence of the individual Assistant Secretary and the confidence that the Secretary and the White House have in him. If, for instance, the Pentagon wished to assign an additional squadron of fighter planes to American bases in Japan, it would have to ask the Department of State to obtain the approval of the Japanese government under the terms of the security treaty. The Assistant Secretary of State for East Asian and Pacific Affairs would be the one to decide whether the internal political situation in Japan was favorable or not, and whether or not to instruct the American Ambassador in Tokyo to consult with the Japanese Foreign Ministry. If he decided that the time was not propitious, the Pentagon could insist by having the Secretary of Defense ask the Secretary of State to overrule the Assistant Secretary. But on a question of this order, that is not likely.

The geographic bureaus are the main operating units within the department. They are organized along rather arbitrary and sometimes illogical lines, the reasons for which are lost in bureaucratic obscurity. The Bureau of European Affairs covers the region from

29

the Soviet Union to Portugal and includes Iceland and Canada. The Bureau of African Affairs spans that continent from the shores of the Mediterranean to the Cape of Good Hope, even though North African nations are oriented more toward Europe and the Middle East than to sub-Saharan Africa. The Bureau of East Asian and Pacific Affairs is perhaps more logical, covering China, Korea, Japan, the nations of Southeast Asia, and Australia and New Zealand in the South Pacific. In contrast, the Bureau of Near Eastern and South Asian Affairs runs from Greece, which, the last time anyone looked at a geography book, was in Europe, through Israel and the Arab states to India, Pakistan, and Ceylon. The Bureau of Inter-American Affairs is a hybrid of the State Department and the Agency for International Development that was put together during President Kennedy's administration to administer his Alliance for Progress. The Bureau of International Organizations tends to American interests in the United Nations and other international economic and social organizations.

The principal officers within the bureaus are the Country Directors, sometimes called by their older title, desk officers. They are in charge of the work pertaining to one nation or a small packet of nations. The Country Directors and their staffs of half a dozen or so officers do the daily work of the department—drafting memoranda for their superiors, writing telegrams to embassies abroad, conferring with officials of other bureaus and departments, negotiating with foreign diplomats in Washington, and watching developments in the nation for which they are responsible to make recommendations on changes in American policy or in the handling of problems. Perhaps the most time-consuming task of the Country Director is obtaining the concurrence of other officials on policy papers and telegrams. For instance, the Country Director for Peru drafts a cable to the American Embassy there instructing it to release funds for an agricultural development project. He must then obtain the approval of the Assistant Secretary, the Deputy Coordinator for AID, the general counsel of AID who passes on the legalities, the appropriate officer in the Bureau of Economic

Affairs, and the Office of Regional Economic Policy. This last must obtain clearance from other agencies of government, such as the Department of Agriculture and the Department of Commerce if trade is involved. The Country Director may also check with the Bureau of Congressional Relations if he thinks there may be Congressional interest, the Bureau of Public Affairs if there may be public interest, and the United States Information Agency if it has news value in Latin America. Each official with whom the Country Director confers may suggest modifications and the telegram will be held up until all are agreed on what it says. But it is this control of the paperwork that gives the Country Director a major say in the thousands of invisible problems that must be resolved each year.

Among the staff bureaus, the Assistant Secretary for Congressional Relations has perhaps the most obscure and thankless job at the sub-cabinet level in government. Yet it is important. He ostensibly represents the department's view on the Hill when legislation is under consideration. But much more of his time is spent in trying to win or to maintain Congressional support for the foreign policy of the administration in office. Or, put another way, his major responsibility is to prevent opposition to the administration's foreign policy from crystallizing within the Congress, both on specific issues and on the general tenor of that policy.

The responsibilities of the other staff Assistant Secretaries are evident from the titles of their bureaus. The Bureau of International Scientific and Technological Affairs deals with other governments on space, the environment, and atomic energy. The Bureau of Intelligence and Research analyzes information from embassies and intelligence agencies and distills that for the Secretary and the Assistant Secretaries. The Bureau of Economic Affairs handles negotiations on commerce, monetary questions, trade, transport, and communications. The Bureau of Public Affairs explains foreign policy through publications, speakers, and conferences. The Bureau of Educational and Cultural Affairs handles exchanges with other governments in those fields. A relatively new bureau, the Bureau of Politico-Military Affairs reflects the weight of American military power in foreign policy and acts as a liaison office between the State Department and the Department of Defense, particulary with the Office of International Security Affairs in the Pentagon.

Overseas, the American embassies are the eyes, ears, and fingertips of the government. The ambassador, while the personal representative of the President, reports on routine questions to the Secretary of State through a Country Director and an Assistant Secretary. The ambassador and his staff provide information for policy decisions, make recommendations on policy, and carry it out after he has been instructed to do so. But the role of the ambassador has been diluted in the past quarter-century because modern transport and communications are so efficient. He operates under close instructions from Washington and little is left to his discretion. Senior officers often travel from Washington to handle particularly important negotiations or to give an agreement more prestige by going to the foreign capital to be present for its final approval. Secretaries of State have become more involved in government-to-government negotiations in recent years, with John Foster Dulles probably holding the record for the most travel. In the Nixon Administration, the President made wide use of special emissaries, including cabinet officers, to negotiate with other governments, often completely bypassing the State Department and the embassy abroad. Secretary of the Treasury John B. Connally, most notably, was the key figure in obtaining the realignment of major currencies in late 1971. Although that economic issue had immense diplomatic implications, the State Department and the diplomatic service were only marginally involved.

On the other hand, the ambassador's authority has been enhanced in his role as head of the "country team" that includes representatives of all other American agencies in the host country except senior military officers in charge of separate commands. They are responsible to their service chiefs and to the Joint Chiefs of Staff. The ambassador is responsible for coordinating the recommendations that go back to Washington and for coordinating the instructions that come out from Washington. He is charged with seeing that the various agencies do not work at cross-purposes, a mandate first given by President Kennedy when he feared that the Central Intelligence Agency and perhaps others were going in different directions. Thus, the ambassador has become something of a diplomatic executive, although that role has not been fully developed. As in Washington itself, much depends on the style, the personality, and the bureaucratic ability of the ambassador to exert leadership with the representatives of the diverse interests in his embassy or country team.

4

Across the River

IN HIS CUMBERSOME but classic treatise *On War,* General Karl Maria von Clausewitz wrote that "war is nothing but a continuation of political intercourse, with a mixture of other means." The Prussian theoretician, writing in the 1820's after the Napoleonic Wars, asked rhetorically: "Does the cessation of diplomatic notes stop the political relations between different nations and governments? Is not war merely another kind of writing and language from political thoughts? It has certainly a grammar of its own, but its logic is not peculiar to itself."

Von Clausewitz decreed that military power be subordinated to politics in foreign policy. He wrote:

That the political point of view should end completely when war begins is only conceivable in contests which are wars of life and death, from pure hatred: As wars are in reality, they are, as we said before, only the expressions or manifestations of policy itself. The subordination of the political point of view to the military would be contrary to common sense, for policy has declared the war; it is the intelligent faculty, war only the instrument, and not the reverse. The subordination of the military point of view to the political is, therefore, the only thing which is possible.

Since World War II, the United States has modified von Clausewitz' doctrine to the point where military power has been given equal, and in some cases greater weight than political policy in the

35

formulation of foreign policy. The strategy of unconditional surrender applied to the Axis Powers in World War II put total emphasis on a military rather than a political resolution of that conflict. In the Korean War, the United States was frustrated in the attempt to find a military victory and was forced to accept a political settlement. But that apparently did not lessen the belief that there are times when military power should receive priority over politics. The Pentagon Papers showed, among other things, how political considerations gradually gave way to an attempted military solution, an effort that eventually failed. With that, the United States tried to return to a political settlement of the conflict —but never wholeheartedly. One of the reasons that the United States has found it difficult to extract itself from Vietnam was the continuing concept that a military rather than a political solution could be found.

Moreover, the threat to the national security of the United States over the last twenty-five years has been fundamentally military. The threat has come from the nuclear power of the Soviet Union; the limited wars in Korea and Vietnam; the nationalist revolutions in the third world that the Soviet Union or Communist China have tried to manipulate to their own benefit; and other struggles that might have involved the United States, such as those between Israel and the Arab states and between India and Pakistan.

With the nuclear powers so far at a standoff, the major threat has been limited war. The Soviet Union and China have refined their doctrines of limited war to a paraphrase of von Clausewitz: "If war is a continuation of politics, only by other means, so also peace is a continuation of struggle, only by other means." Or, as Chairman Mao Tse-tung has put it: "Talk, talk, fight, fight."

Confronted with this, the United States has geared its military and diplomatic machinery to a defensive containment of the Communist military and political thrust. The American military establishment has, perhaps unconsciously, become a politicized provider of national security. Thus, the Department of Defense, with its headquarters in the Pentagon across the Potomac River from the

Department of State, has come to have an influence in certain critical foreign policy decisions equal to and sometimes greater than that of the State Department.

American relations with at least forty-three nations around the world are founded on an interlocking set of mutual security treaties —the North Atlantic Treaty Organization, the Inter-American Defense Treaty, the Southeast Asia Treaty Organization, the Anzus Treaty with Australia and New Zealand, and bilateral treaties with South Korea, Japan, Taiwan, and the Philippines. Those pacts do much more than set a military alliance; they are the foundation of a myriad of other agreements, political, economic, and cultural. They provide a tone that pervades American policies and actions that concern the other nations, especially in the day-to-day relations between American and foreign official representatives.

The security treaties generally permit the United States to maintain bases and to station troops within the territory of the other signatory. That provides the host nation with a visible American presence and frequently makes an impact on the local economy as Americans officially and personally spend money there. Moreover, the United States has military advisory groups in still more countries. They are particularly influential in developing nations where the military officer corps is a major political force. The contacts between American advisers and those officers give the advisers an opportunity for influence greater than that of American diplomats in many cases. All told, the nearly two million American military men and women spread across the face of the globe collectively and individually constitute America in the minds of millions of people and their governments. Sometimes they are representatives of goodwill, as during the relief operations in East Pakistan after a ravaging cyclone hit in November, 1970. American helicopter crews flew tons of supplies to help two and a half million homeless and starving people to survive. At other times, unhappily, there are frictions. An American general in Korea once lamented: "Most of my troops think the Koreans are filthy whores or slicky-boys [thieves]. Most of the Koreans think the average GI is a loud drunken sex-fiend. Yet they're all pretty decent people. It's too bad they can't see the good side of each other."

The impact of the military on the making of foreign policy in Washington is perhaps best seen in the federal budget. The Defense Department's budget in 1970 took about one-third of all federal expenditures. The size of that allocation alone gave the department immense weight in the decision-making process since it represented a priority over domestic departments and other agencies engaged in foreign affairs. The military establishment is a huge, cumbersome organization caught in an endless race to keep up with the development of new weapons systems and all manner of military technology. It must plan one, five, and ten years ahead and once those programs are begun they are difficult to stop. Thus, force structures, the deployment of men and the positioning of arms, and a multitude of contingency plans set a pattern that imposes itself on the nation's diplomacy and often makes diplomatic moves respond to it rather than the other way around.

When President Nixon promulgated the Nixon Doctrine in 1970, the burden of implementing it fell primarily on the Pentagon since the major element of the doctrine was the reduction of American military power in East Asia. The most prominent feature, of course, was the gradual withdrawal of American forces from South Vietnam. But along with that went a reduction in forces in South Korea, the return of Okinawa to Japan, a cut in American bases and forces in Japan, a cutback in the Seventh Fleet in the Western Pacific, a consolidation of bases in the Philippines, and a cut in forces in Thailand. Each of those military moves caused political problems that American diplomats had to negotiate with the host governments.

The Secretary of Defense, as with any other cabinet officer, is the single most influential man in determining what impact his department makes on policy. Much depends on the confidence the President places in him and on his relationship with the Secretary of State and, to a lesser extent, with other officers of government such as the Director of Central Intelligence or the Chairman of the

Atomic Energy Commission. Under President Truman, Secretary of State Acheson was clearly more influential than the erratic Secretary of Defense, Louis Johnson, with whom Mr. Acheson had a running feud. When General Marshall became Secretary of Defense, he and Mr. Acheson worked in harmony and were equally influential with the President. Under President Eisenhower, the chief architect of foreign policy was Secretary of State John Foster Dulles rather than Secretary of Defense Charles Wilson. With President Kennedy, Secretary of Defense Robert S. McNamara rather quickly moved into a position of more telling influence than Secretary of State Rusk. But that shifted when President Johnson took office and as Mr. McNamara gradually began to question the wisdom of the American involvement in Vietnam. Mr. Rusk consistently favored President Johnson's strong military action in Vietnam—Washington gossip held him to be more the Secretary of Defense than the Secretary of State. Under President Nixon, Secretary of Defense Melvin R. Laird brought to his office his long experience with military affairs as a Representative in the Congress and rapidly gained a greater voice in foreign policy than did the inexperienced Secretary of State, Mr. Rogers. Mr. Laird shared President Nixon's general views on the nature of the threats to American national security. He was, further, a political power in his own right, unlike most of his predecessors, and that gave his words even more importance.

The Secretary of Defense exercises his influence primarily through the NSC, where he expresses the Pentagon point of view in contention or in conjuction with that of the Secretary of State. Below that, the Defense perspective comes into the decision-making process through the Deputy Secretary's membership on the main subordinate committees and the presence of a Defense Department representative in the Interdepartmental Groups, the working groups, and the ad hoc task forces. In addition, military officers and Defense Department civilian officials are posted for tours of duty at the State Department to provide a ready reference on Pentagon thinking, just as foreign service officers are on duty in the Pentagon.

Within the Pentagon, the Joint Chiefs of Staff, the Office of International Security Affairs, and the Defense Review Committee are three elements of particular importance to the making of foreign policy.

The Joint Chiefs of Staff, established by the National Security Act of 1947 as the nation's senior military council, comprise a chairman appointed by the President and rotated through the Army, Navy, and Air Force, the Army Chief of Staff, the Chief of Naval Operations, and the Air Force Chief of Staff. When matters pertaining to the Marine Corps are under consideration, the Commandant of the Corps sits in. The Joint Chiefs wear two hats, one as the President's principal military advisers, another as the Secretary of Defense's military advisers. The distinction is important since legally the Joint Chiefs have direct access to the President on military matters or on political issues that bear on the military posture of the United States. While the Chairman of the JCS is not a statutory member of the NSC, he is an adviser to it. In addition, each Chief of Staff has operational control over his service. Thus, their advice and recommendations up the line and their orders down the line have a marked influence on national security policy. Laterally, the military chiefs can bring pressures to bear through their advocates on Capitol Hill. The Armed Services Committees of the House and Senate have generally been disposed to accept the views of the JCS on policy and, more important, appropriations and to adopt them for their own. In recent years, however, the Congress in general has been less well disposed toward the military and has insisted on cuts in the military budget.

The Office of International Security Affairs (ISA), headed by an Assistant Secretary of Defense, is the foreign policy staff for the Secretary of Defense. It is responsible for the research and analysis on international problems that affect the military posture of the United States and for making recommendations to the Secretary. It is also the main liaison office with the State Department and other agencies engaged in foreign affairs. Further, ISA supervises the important military assistance program, which strongly affects the diplomatic relations of the United States with the recipient nation. Some equipment and weapons are given away, while other supplies are sold at reduced prices out of surplus stocks. By 1970 that had gotten to be such a large program that some Congressmen objected to it. They argued that the Pentagon, by determining on its own authority which nations would receive arms and which would not, was conducting a vital part of American foreign policy without Congressional approval.

ISA is staffed with both civilian and military officials, usually with a civilian as deputy assistant secretary and as head of each of the main branches while a general is his second in command. Four of the deputy assistant secretaries head geographic sections such as European and NATO Affairs, and East Asian and Pacific Affairs. Another official is charged with policy planning and is the main channel for communication with the NSC staff in the White House. Still another large section, headed by a lieutenant general, is responsible for military sales and assistance.

The Defense Program Review Committee, which is actually part of the NSC system, is a relatively new unit that was established by President Nixon in 1969. The President, who named his Assistant for National Security Affairs as chairman, outlined the committee's duties in his message to the Congress on foreign policy in February, 1970. He said:

"This permanent committee reviews major defense, fiscal, policy and program issues in terms of their strategic, diplomatic, political and economic implications and advises me and the National Security Council on its findings." The committee was charged with examining major areas, such as weapons systems and the size and organization of the armed forces, and relating their cost to the diplomatic and domestic needs of the nation. The President said: "Our great wealth and productive capacity still do not enable us to pursue every worthwhile national objective with unlimited means. Choices among defense strategies and budgets have a great

41

impact on the extent to which we can pursue other national goals."

A good illustration of the impact of the military on foreign policy was President Nixon's decision to send American troops into Cambodia in May, 1970. It affected the administration's posture on a negotiated settlement of the war in Vietnam, brought into question the President's intent to carry out the policy expressed in the Nixon Doctrine, and triggered a swift increase in political dissension within the United States. It was also a decision showing that, despite the emphasis in the Nixon Administration on orderly process in established institutions, many decisions of foreign policy are made through a process that is improvised as it goes along.

For several years before the incursion, American military leaders in Saigon had wanted to go after North Vietnamese sanctuaries in the eastern provinces of Cambodia. Those safe havens lay at the end of the Ho Chi Minh trail, a web of paths and roads that started in North Vietnam, cut through the jungles of southern Laos, and spread into Cambodia and South Vietnam. The North Vietnamese had built up headquarters, communications centers, supply depots, hospitals, and rest areas throughout the sanctuaries. From those bases, Communist forces slipped into South Vietnam for quick forays or sustained combat and then returned to safety.

Diplomatic and domestic political considerations had precluded open attacks on the sanctuaries. The United States wanted to avoid intensifying an unpopular war, to avoid provoking the Communist Chinese into the war, to avoid complicating the already unproductive peace talks in Paris, and to avoid more international criticism of American policy in Southeast Asia.

Then, in March, 1970, Prince Norodom Sihanouk, the volatile but shrewd head of the Cambodian government, was overthrown in a military coup. He was replaced by General Lon Nol, an event that was seen by senior military officers in Saigon and Washington as an opportunity to override diplomatic constraints and go after the sanctuaries. But so long as the North Vietnamese made no overt moves against Lon Nol, the previous policy stood.

The North Vietnamese, however, began to stir. They saw potential danger in Lon Nol's hostility toward their forces in the eastern provinces. In a matter of weeks, they hardened their diplomatic attitude toward his government, moved troops to stave off probes by Cambodian troops, and finally threatened to take over all of Cambodia by force. Lon Nol asked for aid, which American military leaders in Saigon recommended he be given. They also recommended that American and South Vietnamese forces be permitted to try to knock out the North Vietnamese bases in Cambodia.

That request led to the decision, made during the last ten days of April, to go into Cambodia. The President met first with the NSC to discuss the general situation, then asked the Washington Special Action Group, one of the NSC subordinate committees, to outline the options open to him. It came up with alternatives ranging from modest military assistance to Lon Nol, through an invasion by South Vietnamese troops with American advisers and air support, to a combined invasion of South Vietnamese and American forces with armor, artillery, and air support.

The President next consulted separately and collectively with key advisers in a forum that was informal and put together solely for that decision. From Defense came Secretary Laird and General Earle G. Wheeler, the Chairman of the JCS; from State, Secretary Rogers; from intelligence, Director of Central Intelligence Richard Helms; on political aspects, Attorney General John H. Mitchell and White House aides John D. Ehrlichman and H.R. Haldeman. A key man was Dr. Kissinger, the President's Assistant for National Security Affairs, who arranged meetings, organized the staff work, chaired the Special Action Group, presented the options to the President, and relayed his instructions to the rest of the government.

One other key adviser was in Saigon. That was General Creighton W. Abrams, the American commander there. Just before making his final decision, the President sent a telegram to the General directly, without going through the usual channels. He asked the General to give his assessment man-to-man and with unvarnished truth, saying that the reply would count greatly in the ultimate decision. General Abrams replied that the assault was necessary to protect American troops and to go forward with plans for withdrawing and turning the war over to the South Vietnamese. He gave assurances of a reasonable chance of success.

It is interesting to note who was left out of the decision-making process. Vice President Agnew and the Director of the Office of Emergency Preparedness, George A. Lincoln, both statutory members of the NSC, did not participate after the first NSC discussion. The subordinate committees of the NSC, other than the Special Action Group, were bypassed. No one other than Secretary of State Rogers and Undersecretary for Political Affairs U. Alexis Johnson, a member of the Special Action Group, was consulted in the Department of State. The decision was made by the President on recommendations from military commanders and with the advice only of the President's closest advisers.

General Abrams' advice tipped the balance. The President himself favored strong military action. Mr. Laird and General Wheeler felt the same but were reluctant to commit American ground troops. Mr. Mitchell warned that an incursion was required but said that it would have an adverse political reaction in the United States—a reaction that he underestimated. Mr. Rogers was against the incursion on grounds that it would damage diplomatic efforts to negotiate an end to the war. Dr. Kissinger, so far as could be ascertained, kept his thoughts to himself and saw his role as a staff assistant to present choices to the President and to see that the President's orders were carried out.

The diplomatic and political consequences of the Cambodian incursion were multiple. Negotiations with the North Vietnamese in Paris, which were already bogged down, came to a halt. A hint from the Soviet Union that Communist nations might be willing to participate in a new Geneva Conference to settle all of the issues in Southeast Asia also went into a deep freeze. Leaders of many nations in Asia concluded, incorrectly, that President Nixon's doctrine for the reduction of American military power in Asia was a paper exercise. President Nixon intended, how successfully is unknown, to demonstrate to Russian and Chinese leaders that he could be tough if pushed. He wanted them to understand that he was ready to negotiate issues such as a limitation on strategic arms and the Middle East crisis but that he was determined to do it on what he considered realistic grounds. Domestically, the Cambodian venture shattered the fragile standoff the administration had achieved with the war dissenters. There were demonstrations across the country, moratoriums in many universities, and outbursts of political activity in the halls of Congress.

All of this resulted from one operation that, in purely military terms, was relatively small in scale and short in duration. But it showed the penetrating effect that one such military decision could have on foreign policy and domestic politics. Defenders of the administration argued that it was militarily necessary because it gave the United States the time and space needed to withdraw from Vietnam safely. But that argument had little effect diplomatically or politically.

5

The Second Oldest Profession

THE BIBLE says that the Lord instructed Moses, while the Israelites were wandering in the desert, to "send thou men, that they may spy out the land of Canaan." Moses therefore dispatched twelve men into Canaan with these instructions: "Get you up this way by the South, and go into the hill-country and see the land, what it is; and the people that dwell therein, whether they are strong or weak, whether they are few or many; and what the land is that they dwell in, whether it is good or bad; and what cities they are that they dwell in, whether in camps, or in strongholds; and what the land is, whether it is fat or lean, whether there is wood therein, or not. And be ye of good courage, and bring of the fruit of the land."

Now one of the spies was Joshua, who later became a general. He apparently learned his lessons well, since before he fought the battle of Jericho he sent two spies into the city to the house of Rahab, the harlot, where they were hidden. When the King of Jericho discovered that the spies were in the city, Rahab lowered them on a rope out of the window of her house, which sat on the wall of the city. They evaded the search party that had been sent after them, reported back to Joshua, and he went on to lay siege to Jericho and to capture it.

Harlotry may be the world's oldest profession but the gathering of intelligence lays claim to being a close second. Moses and Joshua sent spies to find out what the opposition was capable of doing, what it was actually doing, and what it might intend to do. They used that information to make their own plans and to carry them out. The reasons for collecting information today are no different. Only the extent and the techniques have changed. The United States spends between $3 billion and $6 billion a year to determine the capabilities, actions, and intentions of friend, neutral, and foe. American intelligence studies politics, economics, military power, technical skill, social trends, and a myriad of other fields. The information is gathered from newspapers and radio broadcasts, from diplomatic reports and tourists, from sophisticated electronic and photographic equipment on planes and ships and satellites, and from undercover agents who are the professional descendants of Joshua and his eleven colleagues. The information is analyzed by human specialists and electronic computers and turned into estimates that officials from the President to the most obscure bureaucrat use in deciding the foreign policy of the nation and the actions that will be taken to realize it.

Good, hard facts and clever analysis of clues, plus sound interpretation, is the stuff of intelligence. Unfortunately, much of that is overlooked by the public since the headlines in the press, the melodramas on television, and the thrills of spy novels tend to focus on "dirty tricks" such as political subversion, sabotage, and assassination. Glamorous—or infamous—as those operations are, they are not really the reason a nation maintains an intelligence service. Someone once said that information is power. He might have cogently added that this is the fundamental motivation behind gathering information and processing it into intelligence. Much of intelligence work is tedious, much requires painstaking patience, and most of it is never exposed to the public. But it provides the daily ration on which policy-makers feed for their very existence.

Before World War II, American military intelligence broke the

Japanese diplomatic code in an operation called MAGIC, enabling President Roosevelt and Secretary of State Cordell Hull to read Japanese proposals before they were officially presented. (That they may have misread Japanese intentions by taking the messages out of context, as some observers have maintained, was possibly a good example of solid intelligence work gone awry.) During the war, a German named Richard Sorge was secretly a Communist and a Soviet agent—and a close friend of the German ambassador in Tokyo. From him Sorge elicited information that Germany's Japanese allies had no intention of massing an attack on the Soviet Union across the border of Manchuria. That allowed the Russians to concentrate their forces on the European front to defeat the Germans. In the late 1950's, the United States got valuable information from the overflights of the U-2, a high-altitude powered glider equipped with advanced cameras and film. After that operation was discredited when Francis Gary Powers was shot down in 1960, the United States switched to spy-in-the-sky satellites over the Soviet Union and presumably the Soviets did the same over the United States. The U-2 went on, however, to produce invaluable photographs of Soviet missile sites in Cuba during the crisis of 1962. Later, seaborne electronic snooping came to light when Israeli planes strafed the American ship *Liberty* in the Mediterranean Sea during the Six-Day war in 1967 and when the North Koreans captured a similar ship, *Pueblo,* off their coast in 1968.

Operations such as those grab the news headlines and reinforce a popular notion that intelligence is an exciting, if nefarious, game of cloak and dagger in the hidden ways of John Le Carre's *Spy Who Came in from the Cold* or Ian Fleming's James Bond. There is some of that—but precious little when compared with the immense amount of information that is gathered from a variety of sources in a routine and often humdrum manner.

Intelligence, by definition, is raw information that has been analyzed and pieced together with other bits of information into a report that has meaning and is useful to officials making policy and plans. Intelligence estimates can be strategic—what is the state of

49

Soviet technology and therefore the ability to turn out nuclear missiles? It can be tactical—what are the signs that the North Vietnamese plan a major offensive? It can be political—what changes did the resignation of President Charles de Gaulle of France portend on the attitude of the French government toward NATO? Intelligence can be economic—what effect does tension in the Middle East have on the world oil supply and therefore on fuel supplies in the United States? It can be social—what trends in a developing nation such as Indonesia will affect that nation's foreign policies? It can be scientific and technical—what is the quality of Chinese education in physics and therefore that nation's capacity for developing a nuclear strike force? Intelligence can be personal —what is the state of North Korean Premier Kim Il Sung's health and how will that affect his judgment toward South Korea? Any particular intelligence report is likely to be a combination of a number of those elements as the analyst tries to figure out all of the variables that will bear on the policy and posture of the government. In all of this, measuring capability and actions is easier than gauging intentions, for intentions include human motivations that are surely among the least predictable things in the world.

The information that is processed into intelligence comes from overt, covert, and technical sources. American diplomats and embassy attachés abroad overtly obtain information from officials of the host country, ruling and opposition politicians, intellectuals, businessmen, labor leaders, and the local press. Foreign correspondence in the American press is another overt source. Newsmen, not bound by the niceties of diplomacy, are frequently more free to inquire into the politics, economics, and life of another nation than are diplomats. Their dispatches sometimes reach the United States faster than the cables of diplomats, who are encumbered by bureaucratic red tape. Foreign publications of all sorts are a major overt source of information, even in totalitarian nations. Dictatorships, which maintain strict controls over the press, use the news media to tell their people what they want them to know and what they want them to do. A careful analyst can discern from that a government's policy on a specific question or its general attitude on various issues or its problems. Exhortations to workers to increase steel production, for instance, are a sure sign that the steel industry is having troubles. Newspapers, journals, and radio broadcasts have long been staples for the Kremlinologist and the China-watcher.

A covert source is a technical name for a spy. Some operate under what is known in the espionage trade as shallow-cover. They pose as officials of the American Embassy or the Agency for International Development without changing their names and identity or undertaking an elaborate ruse to make themselves appear as private persons. The opposite is a deep-cover agent, who assumes a new name and identity and establishes himself as a businessman or scholar or in some other capacity to conceal completely his connection with the American government. Some deep-cover agents are citizens of the nation on which they are spying. They may oppose the government in power there or be sympathetic to the aims of the United States, or they may simply be people whose services can be bought.

The fastest-growing and most sophisticated sources of information today are technical. The United States monitors radio stations all over the world and, secretly, listens to diplomatic and military messages hoping to break the codes in which they are written. Satellites carry sensing devices that watch for the tell-tale streak of heat that a missile in flight leaves behind. Listening devices and long-range directional microphones are used to pick up secret conversations among diplomats, politicians, and anyone else who might provide critical information. Photographic intelligence has reached a high state of art. The U-2 aircraft that took the pictures of Cuban missile sites in 1962 were acclaimed as technical marvels. But intelligence officials connected with the development of the U-2 said that the truly great advance was in secret research done to make the cameras and films that would provide clear, detailed pictures from heights of fifteen miles.

The producers of the immense flow of information into the decision-making process in Washington are the agencies in what is

51

known as the intelligence community. It comprises the Central Intelligence Agency, the Defense Intelligence Agency, the National Security Agency, parts of the State Department, the intelligence services of the Army, Navy, and Air Force, plus intelligence functions within the Atomic Energy Commission, the Treasury, the Department of Justice (primarily the Federal Bureau of Investigation), the National Aeronautics and Space Administration, and other agencies. Each is supposed to concentrate on particular types of information but there is considerable overlap, duplication, and competition. Each performs at least two separate functions, one being the collection and reporting of information, the other the analysis and processing of information into intelligence.

At the center of the intelligence community is the Central Intelligence Agency, which was established under the National Security Act of 1947 as the successor to the wartime Office of Strategic Services. The Director of Central Intelligence is the government's senior intelligence officer, the President's adviser on intelligence, and an adviser to the National Security Council. Allen W. Dulles, who served as the agency's third director from 1953 to 1962, was generally given credit for putting it on its feet. Mr. Dulles, brother of Secretary of State John Foster Dulles, ran the agency with a free hand and was criticized for taking it beyond the intelligence field into the making of policy. His successor, the scholarly John A. McCone, who had been chairman of the AEC, gradually pulled the agency out of policy matters. The most recent director, Richard Helms, who was appointed in 1967, was the first to have been a career official of CIA and to have risen through the ranks. Mr. Helms was known in Washington to have deliberately kept the agency out of policy matters. His practice, to paraphrase Jack Webb's television character Sergeant Joe Friday, was just to give the facts.

Besides being the focal point of intelligence analysis, the CIA is responsible for collecting and preparing its own reports. The agency has four main operating branches. The Division of Plans is the most secret as it runs deep-cover agents, seeks out informers, and tries to persuade key Communist officials to defect. It has had agents dig tunnels under the Berlin Wall into East Berlin to tap telephone cables running from the Soviet military headquarters there, an agent in Poland acquire a copy of former Soviet Premier Nikita Khrushchev's famous secret speech in which he denounced his predecessor, Joseph Stalin, in 1956, and agents run an airline known as Air America to serve as a transport and communication channel for CIA operations all over Asia. More important are the scores of agents in every country around the world who rarely tap a phone, rarely steal a document (though they might photograph some), and rarely have any of the exciting adventures that are shown on television dramas. Instead, they lead quiet lives in as routine and unobtrusive a manner as possible, working at jobs and raising families in a way that arouses no suspicion. Gradually they work themselves into positions as minor bureaucrats or business executives where they pick up immense amounts of information either in little scraps or in great doses and send it secretly to Washington. It is that steady stream of information that provides the real grist for the intelligence analyst and his computer and files.

The CIA's Division of Intelligence assembles, collates, and tries to make sense of all of the information that comes in from covert, overt, and technical sources. Like the Department of State, it is divided into geographic offices that watch developments in particular countries. Those offices are staffed with specialists of every sort —political scientists, economists, sociologists, a variety of scientists. It is their job to study the information that comes in and to relay to officials reports and estimates of what is going on all over the world. Their headquarters is a large, modernistic building set in the woods in Langley, Virginia, across the Potomac River northwest of Washington.

The Division of Science and Technology is responsible for keeping abreast of nuclear, technical, and similar developments in foreign nations and for interpreting the results of technical and electronic operations mounted by American intelligence. The Division of Support handles procurement, communications security, and personnel.

The Defense Intelligence Agency, established by Secretary of Defense Robert S. McNamara in 1961, is charged with coordinating the activities of Army, Navy, and Air Force Intelligence. It sets requirements, much as a newspaper editor gives a reporter an assignment, and analyzes the information that comes back from the military intelligence services. Mr. McNamara set up the agency to give his office and the Defense Department an independent source of intelligence that specialized in military affairs and on events that bore particularly on the military posture of the United States. Much of that is what is known as "order of battle" intelligence—the disposition, armament, quality of training and leadership, and logistic support in the military forces of other nations. It includes technical and weapons developments among those foreign military services. Until early 1971, DIA reported to the Joint Chiefs of Staff. But Secretary Laird ordered it to report directly to him in a move intended to give him greater control over it, more influence within the intelligence community, and more say in foreign policy decisions.

The intelligence services of the Army, Navy, and Air Force are primarily operational arms that collect information through military attachés in American embassies abroad, through shallow-cover and some deep-covert agents, and through electronic, sensing, and other technical devices. But each service has an assistant chief of staff for intelligence in the Pentagon with a small staff to undertake analytical tasks to keep the heads of the three services informed on developments abroad, especially tactical movements, that affect their services.

The National Security Agency, with its headquarters at Ft. Meade, Maryland, is probably the most expensive, technically sophisticated, and greatest employer in the American intelligence community. Its task is listening to diplomatic, military, and other radio traffic around the world, trying to break codes or to develop a reading of what is happening by the volume and direction of messages sent. NSA also provides some guidance for similar electronic operations by the military intelligence services. Besides collecting the information, it collates and assembles it into analytical reports for policy makers.

Elsewhere, specialists in the Department of State's Intelligence and Research Bureau prepare analyses from information supplied by diplomats abroad; the Atomic Energy Commission, with its technical and scientific expertise, watches nuclear developments around the world; the Treasury has agents and informants whose main task is to inform the Customs service; the Justice Department's agents report on narcotics developments abroad; the National Aeronautics and Space Administration keeps tabs on other nations' space and rocketry developments; the Departments of Commerce, Labor, and Agriculture are sources of information on economic developments overseas.

The amount of information and intelligence produced by all of those agencies is immense. CIA alone has between 100 and 150 items pouring in every hour, every day. Most of it is fed into computer storage banks, dossiers, and files for later use since only a small portion is of immediate interest. The most urgent and most important is put into a paper for the President each morning. The Secretaries of State and Defense are similarly briefed each day. During the day, the most important current items are fed into the operations rooms at the White House, the State Department, and the Pentagon.

But the bulk of the material is studied by specialists who write analytical papers for policy planners at every level. One such study might be a report on Soviet naval strength, showing the overall numbers of Russian warships and where they have been moved in a particular period and, especially, why. In recent years, the Soviet Union has shown signs of becoming a major naval power, first with a buildup in the Mediterranean, then the Atlantic and Caribbean, after that in East Asia operating from Vladivostok, and finally in the Indian Ocean. Another study might be an intensive look at the political, economic, and social factors that affect the Japanese negotiating position on textiles. It would go to officials in the White House, the Department of Commerce, and the State Department who are either involved in or guiding the bargaining.

Still longer reports are known as National Intelligence Estimates. They are produced by a staff within the CIA that draws on the resources of the entire intelligence community and are reviewed and approved by the National Intelligence Board, which is headed by the Director of Central Intelligence. Those studies set out the long-term trends in a particular country and are the basis for long-term policy decisions on United States relations with them. Studies are also made of specific questions, such as the state of nuclear arms and nuclear power around the world. Although the members of the intelligence community and the board try to reach a consensus on the estimate, that rarely happens. Each agency, however, is permitted to register its dissent and its own view in the report so that the policy-maker, whether it be the President or a bureaucrat, can see that there are uncertainties.

One other aspect of the intelligence game, and one that receives considerable public attention, is what is known as "dirty tricks." That includes propaganda from hidden sources, such as a clandestine radio station; political manipulation such as bribery, subversion, and assassination; and unconventional, paramilitary operations such as sabotage and guerrilla warfare. In the strictest sense, however, those are not intelligence operations, even though they are performed by the CIA and other operational intelligence services. They are, rather, users of intelligence in the same manner as the less sinister user in the Department of Commerce preparing for a textile negotiation. Dirty tricks are, or at least should be, the result of a policy decision, not an element that leads to one.

There have been occasions, however, when subversive operations have forced a policy decision. Perhaps the most notable was the Bay of Pigs invasion of Cuba in 1961 shortly after President Kennedy came to office. The impetus for that venture came from the CIA and the Pentagon, who had Cuban exiles ready to go before the President and his administration had decided what their policy toward Cuba would be. After the debacle of defeat, it became evident that the cart had been put before the horse and steps were taken to preclude similar ventures in the future. Whether they can be prevented depends on the grasp that elected political leaders have on the intelligence bureaucracy and on how responsive and responsible senior bureaucrats are to political authority.

6

Little
State Departments

ON THE EVENING of August 15, 1971, President Nixon went on nationwide television to announce his new economic policy. It included three basic elements: the imposition of temporary wage and price controls, the imposition of a 10 percent surtax on imports from abroad, and the suspension of the convertibility of the dollar into gold, also known as "floating" the dollar.

Two of the three elements were momentous foreign policy decisions. The 10 percent surtax was intended to slow down the flow of imports into the American market and the floating of the dollar was intended to reduce the value of the dollar and thereby reduce the cost of American products in world markets.

In the ensuing months, the new economic policy dominated much of American foreign policy. The major executor in this, however, was not the Secretary of State but the Secretary of the Treasury, John B. Connally. He traveled extensively abroad, negotiating with heads of government and finance ministers in an effort to resolve the many economic problems, such as a realignment of international currency values, that had been brought about by the new economic policy. A major overhaul of those currency rates was finally agreed upon in Washington in late December, 1971, and a start was made toward resolving some of the trade questions and rebuilding the international monetary system, which was fundamental to continued trade and foreign investment expansion.

Assisting Secretary Connally in that effort was a relatively small staff headed by John R. Petty, the Assistant Secretary of the Treasury for International Affairs. He headed what was, in effect, a little State Department in the Treasury. Among his staff were career bureaucrats who specialized in international monetary affairs, trade, gold, and foreign exchange, plus men who looked after the United States economic relations with industrialized and developing nations.

Similarly, in the Department of Commerce in 1971 was a capable civil servant named Rauer H. Meyer, who was Director of the Office of Export Control in the Bureau of International Commerce, a major division of the department. As one of the fifty senior bureaucrats in the department he was well known inside the government and among the nation's businessmen engaged in foreign trade. Several Congressmen and members of their staffs knew him from correspondence or from testimony he had given in Congressional hearings. But few ambassadors in Washington had ever heard of him and rarely, if ever, did he get his name in the newspapers.

Yet Mr. Meyer had his hands on an important lever in the foreign policy machinery. His office was charged with implementing the laws and the intricate regulations that controlled the export of American goods to Communist countries. While that may seem mundane when compared with the confrontations between the United States and Communist powers in Southeast Asia, the Middle East, Berlin, and on the nuclear front, trade is nonetheless a major element in foreign policy. The United States has used trade policy since the beginning of the Cold War to put pressure on Communist nations or to negotiate with them. The severity of export controls that were applied to each was a good indicator of the degree of enmity in which each was seen by the United States. Thus, by 1970, the United States had relaxed its restrictions on trade with Yugoslavia and several other Eastern European nations, had a fairly tight policy on shipments to the Soviet Union, and an almost total embargo on trade with Communist China.

When the Nixon Administration came to office in January, 1969, the Communist Chinese had already signaled that they wished to explore a slight relaxation of tensions with the United States. The new administration missed the signals at first, then picked them up and responded with two seemingly trivial but politically significant moves. In July and December, 1969, American restrictions on trade with China were eased ever so slightly. That in turn led to the resumption of private talks, after a lapse of two years, between the American and Chinese ambassadors in Warsaw. The United States further indicated its willingness to improve relations with Peking in March, 1970, by removing most of the restrictions on Americans who wished to travel to China. They had been in effect since the Korean War. At the same time, the Nixon Administration quietly decided to put trade with China on the same basis as that with the Soviet Union. The decision was not announced but was held in abeyance until a signal came from the Chinese that they also wished to improve relations. The gentle moves toward opening up communications with Peking, however, were interrupted in the spring of 1970, when President Nixon ordered American troops into Cambodia. The Chinese responded by breaking off the Warsaw talks again. The situation was stagnant for a year. Then an American Ping-Pong team, in Japan for a tournament, was suddenly invited to visit China. The administration quickly gave its blessing. In addition, several American news correspondents were allowed into China for the first time since American reporters were expelled when the Communists came to power in 1949. Shortly after, the United States announced that restrictions on trade with China would be markedly lessened, thus putting into effect a decision that had been made a year earlier. Exchange controls were also relaxed. Meantime, in greatest secrecy, the President was in direct communication with the Chinese leaders in Peking. He sent his Assistant for National Security Affairs, Dr. Kissinger, into China via Pakistan to confer with Premier Chou En-lai of China in early July, 1971. Then, on July 15, the President dramatically announced on television that he himself planned to visit Peking. After another trip by Dr. Kissinger to Peking, and more negotiation, the President went to the Chinese capital on February 21, 1972.

None of the decisions on trade really meant much for trade itself. But they illustrated the importance of trade as a signaling device in American foreign policy. The reading of Peking's intentions all along the way came from the Department of State's specialists in Chinese affairs, as did the recommendations that the United States respond with signals in trade. But the bureaucratic decisions were made in an interdepartmental committee of representatives from Commerce, the Treasury, Defense, State, and the Central Intelligence Agency. Mr. Meyer and his deputy, Sherman R. Abrahamson, were the key men at the working level. On instructions from the committee, they looked over their regulations, studied the list of 2,829 items under commodity controls, and came up with recommendations that were adopted as policy on how to respond to the signals from the Chinese.

Every week, there are hundreds of decisions of varying importance made throughout Washington that affect foreign policy directly or indirectly. Each one by itself might not attract much attention. But taken together, they have a steady and marked influence on foreign policy and especially on economic matters that affect the lives of Americans. The Treasury has an Assistant Secretary of International Affairs who handles problems connected with the balance of payments and the control of foreign assets in the United States. The Department of Agriculture's Assistant Secretary for International Affairs is responsible for American commodity assistance programs under Public Law 480 and for contacts with the United Nations Food and Agricultural Organization. In the Department of Transportation is an Assistant Secretary for Policy and International Affairs charged with solving problems of international air transport. The Atomic Energy Commission licenses technology to other nations for peaceful uses; the Export-

Import Bank promotes foreign trade; the Federal Maritime Commission is involved with questions of international shipping; the National Aeronautics and Space Administration works with space engineers of other nations to broaden the peaceful uses of space. Even the Post Office is involved—it tries to prevent other countries from sending pornographic materials through the mails into the United States. These agencies are so involved in foreign affairs that more than forty have representatives overseas in one place or another.

It is in these departments and agencies that the domestic pressures on foreign policy are most strongly felt. The "Little State Departments" throughout Washington are staffed by bureaucrats more attuned to the domestic scene than to the wider requirements of a complicated foreign policy. They are particularly sensitive to Congressional pressures and to the desires of citizens made known through their representatives on Capitol Hill. To bring some coordination to those sprawling bureaucracies, President Nixon formed an International Economic Council in early 1971. It was intended to draw together the programs of various departments, much as the National Security Council did, into a comprehensive policy.

The impact of departments other than the State Department on diplomacy was amply illustrated in the United States textile dispute with Japan from early 1969 to the fall of 1971. Up to those years, the import of Japanese textiles into the American market caused considerable friction between Japan and America. This friction was reduced in the 1960's through "voluntary" import quotas negotiated between the State Department and the Japanese Foreign Ministry. But when President Nixon was running for office, he promised the textile industry and its spokesmen on Capitol Hill, notably Senator Strom Thurmond of South Carolina, that protection would be extended to imports of textiles made from chemical fibers. Those had been excluded from earlier agreements and the American textile industry, situated largely in the Southern states that Mr. Nixon felt were important to his success at the polls, claimed that imports of those items were hurting it.

The negotiations, however, were not conducted by diplomats in the State Department but by officials of the Department of Commerce who saw the issue mostly in terms of the President's political commitment to Southern Congressmen and to the textile industry. The main negotiator was a Deputy Assistant Secretary of Commerce, Stanley Nehmer, but the Secretary of Commerce, Maurice H. Stans, took a direct interest and in the latter stages of the negotiations assumed personal charge.

After many months of talks, the Americans and Japanese failed to reach agreement. The Americans overlooked a number of noneconomic aspects of the issue, such as rising Japanese nationalism and the feeling that the Americans were still operating in the manner of the post-World War II occupation. The Japanese overlooked the rising protectionist sentiment in the United States and the political pledge made by Mr. Nixon. The problem was complicated by charges, made by the Treasury, that the Japanese were "dumping" television sets on the American market at prices lower than those in Japan itself. The Americans were dissatisfied with Japan's slow pace in reducing restrictions on American exports to Japan and on American investment in Japanese industry. In addition, a restrictive trade bill was introduced in the Congress to put legal barriers on imports of textiles, shoes, and other items. The Secretary of Commerce vigorously supported it for the protection of American industry while the Secretary of State, Mr. Rogers, strongly opposed it because he thought it would damage American relations with Japan, the European Economic Community, and other nations.

Consequently, there loomed the prospect of an economic war between the United States and Japan that professional diplomats on both sides deplored but could do little to avert. They feared that the alliance between Japan and the United States, which provided for political and military cooperation important to both nations, would be disrupted by the bad blood spilled in the name of parochial domestic concerns on each side. In late 1970, President Nixon and Prime Minister Eisaku Sato, wanting to avoid a rupture, agreed that negotiations would resume with both sides making concessions. The President appointed a White House assistant, Peter Flanigan, to conduct the negotiations from a vantage point that would take into account both Mr. Nixon's political commitments and the wider question of United States relations with Japan.

Mr. Flanigan and Nobuhiko Ushiba, the Japanese Ambassador to the United States, came close to an agreement but not close enough to get the American and Japanese textile industries to agree. Then the powerful chairman of the House Ways and Means Committee, Representative Wilbur Mills of Arkansas, made an agreement with Japanese textile manufacturers. But President Nixon, piqued that Mr. Mills had tried to make foreign policy, rejected it. The negotiations were then passed to roving Ambassador David Kennedy, the former Secretary of the Treasury, and his special assistant, Anthony Jurich. They operated under the general supervision of Peter Peterson, the President's assistant for international economic affairs in the White House. Mr. Kennedy and Mr. Jurich finally rammed through an agreement with the Japanese in October, 1971, using tactics such as threatening to impose the Trading with the Enemy Act that made American and Japanese professional diplomats wince. When it was all over, the United States had gained protection for an economically unimportant industry but had put considerable strain into relations with its major ally in Asia. From the Japanese side, much the same could be said. The diplomatic services in both nations had had little to do with the outcome.

In another instance, a precedent for American foreign policy was set in 1970 by the Department of Labor. Since the end of World War II, the United States has been among the leaders in an international effort to devise international organizations to keep the peace and to promote the general welfare of nations. The United Nations, of course, is the best known but there are many others. One is the International Labor Organization, which predates the United Nations and has its roots in the post-World War I League of Nations. The ILO is dedicated to improving working conditions for laboring men around the world. The United States, with its vigorous labor movement, has been an active participant for many years and contributed 25 percent of the funds for its annual budget.

By mid-1970, however, a number of dissatisfactions with the ILO had developed in the American Federation of Labor-Congress of Industrial Organizations, the major American labor federation. Those had been transmitted to the Department of Labor, whose third-ranking officer was the Deputy Undersecretary for International Affairs, George H. Hildebrand. Mr. Hildebrand, along with George Meany, the President of the AFL-CIO, and Edwin P. Neilan, a former president of the United States Chamber of Commerce, were the United States delegates to the ILO. They were particularly aroused by what they considered the improper use of the ILO as a forum for Russian propaganda and the diversion of the ILO from labor matters into international politics.

The resentment boiled over when the newly-elected Director General of the ILO, Wilfred Jenks, a Briton, named a Russian, Pavel E. Astapenko, to be one of the ILO's five Assistant Directors General without consulting the United States. Further, Mr. Jenks insisted on going through with the appointment despite the strong protests of the American delegates. That led Mr. Meany and Mr. Neilan, with Mr. Hildebrand's tacit approval, to demand that the United States Congress cut off the American financial contribution to the ILO. Although the funds had been appropriated by the House of Representatives, they were able to persuade key Senators to come out against the measure and to have it voted down in the Senate. The House, led by Representative John J. Rooney, an abrasive critic of the manner in which the United States spends money abroad, willingly went along with the Senate when the issue came up in a conference to settle differences between the two versions of the bill.

Thus, the United States refused for the first time to pay a financial obligation to an international body to which it was committed by treaty. The State Department opposed the cut on those grounds but lost the argument to the Department of Labor and its allies in the labor movement and Congress. The United States had earlier been highly critical of the Soviet Union, France, and other nations that refused to pay assessments to the United Nations for operations of which they did not approve. The failure of the United States to pay its ILO contribution meant it would no longer be able to contend that other nations had a moral, legal, and treaty responsibility to fulfill their financial obligations to international bodies. While that did not represent the loss of a vital weapon in diplomacy, it was an erosion of a useful position in the constant maneuvering in the international arena.

The Department of Justice gets into foreign affairs through its authority to enforce the anti-trust laws that are intended to prevent excessive concentrations of economic power and to preclude business practices detrimental to the public. Within the Anti-Trust Division of the Justice Department is a Foreign Commerce Section responsible for scrutinizing American business relationships with foreign companies. The major part of its work is advising American companies on actions that might violate the anti-trust laws. The laws of the United States have no validity abroad, of course, but American companies operating overseas and foreign companies wishing to do business in the United States are subject to them.

The Department of Justice filed an anti-trust suit in 1970 against Westinghouse Electric Corporation and two Japanese companies, Mitsubishi Electric Corporation and Mitsubishi Heavy Industries, Ltd., for allegedly conspiring to restrict markets. Attorneys from Justice charged that the American company had illegally agreed with the two Japanese companies that each would not compete in the other's home market. The complaint, filed in a San Francisco district court, claimed that the agreement covered industrial and consumer products ranging from transformers to television sets. The two Mitsubishi companies manufactured the products under license from Westinghouse and the agreement, Justice claimed, was part of the licensing arrangement. The court, at the time of writing, had not given its decision. If Justice won the case, the Mitsubishi companies would be able to make Westinghouse products in Japan at costs lower than Westinghouse itself could in the United States. The Japanese companies would then be able to export those items to America for sale at prices less than those of Westinghouse, which would benefit the American consumer but make business life for Westinghouse more difficult.

A division of the Justice Department that has a direct effect on the lives of Americans is the Bureau of Narcotics and Dangerous Drugs. It is responsible for enforcing the laws against the abuse of drugs and gets into foreign relations in its efforts to stop illegal traffic in drugs. In 1965, the bureau, at the request of the White House, began an effort to stop the raising of opium in Turkey, a source of large quantities of illicit drugs. The bureau sent an official to Ankara to look into the economics of opium growing and found that it was a major cash crop for many farmers. Working through the American ambassador, the official met with Turkish authorities to ask their assistance in cutting down the flow of opium and morphine to France, where it was refined into heroin for shipment to the United States. The largest obstacle was the resistance of the Turks who depended on opium growing for their livelihood.

After three years of negotiation, the United States, represented officially by the embassy and the Agency for International Development, agreed to lend $3.5 million to Turkey. The funds were to be used to pay Turkish farmers to plow the opium poppies under and to turn to other crops. Part of the money was to be spent on new equipment the farmers needed to grow other crops. Still more went to help train the Turkish police in halting the smuggling of opium and morphine. The narcotics bureau further asked the government of France to increase its policing of the illegal laboratories, mostly in Marseille, that made the heroin for export to the United States. The bureau also helped to train French police in anti-narcotics work.

In a similar venture, the bureau sent an official to Mexico, another and closer source of illicit drugs, in an effort to persuade the Mexican government to destroy marijuana fields. When that effort was unsuccessful, a task force of officials from the Treasury's

Bureau of Customs, Justice, State, AID, Defense, the Coast Guard, and the Texas Border Patrol began in 1969 what was known as Operation Intercept. Customs inspectors all along the border between Mexico and the United States stopped Americans and Mexicans—and anyone else—who had previously been allowed to travel freely across the border and searched their cars and baggage for marijuana. That meant delays of four to six hours for travelers, which began to cut into the Mexican tourist trade and brought bitter protest from the Mexican government.

After several weeks, the Mexican government relented and sent a high-level delegation to Washington to negotiate an agreement. Operation Intercept was replaced with Operation Cooperation, under which the Mexican government sought to cut down on the production and shipment of marijuana and the United States relaxed the border inspections. As the operation started to take hold, Attorney General John N. Mitchell issued a statement saying: "Quietly and effectively, the drug enforcement arms of the two governments have driven a wedge into the operating procedures employed by traffickers of marijuana, heroin, cocaine, and other dangerous drugs." Critics of the effort, however, contended that reducing the supply of marijuana led users of drugs to turn to heroin and other hard drugs and thus only intensified the drug problem within the United States. Even in a relatively mundane issue such as this, solving one problem often leads merely to another.

7

High on the Hill

THE CHAIRMAN of the Senate Foreign Relations Committee, J. W. Fulbright, Democrat of Arkansas, opened a hearing of his committee on August 16, 1967, with these remarks:

I believe that a marked constitutional imbalance between the Executive and the Congress in matters of foreign policy has developed in the last twenty-five years as a result of which the Executive has acquired virtually unrestricted power to commit the United States abroad politically and militarily.

I futher believe that this imbalance should be redressed, that it is important for the Congress to reassert a measure of authority in foreign relations, including the war power, the general advise and consent function of the Senate, and the power to pass upon proposed foreign commitments by treaty or other legislative means.

That was an early expression of a desire in the Congress, especially in the Senate, to regain what many on Capitol Hill considered to be their constitutional prerogatives and their political influence in the making of decisions on foreign policy. The attitude expressed by Senator Fulbright caught hold quickly, developed into a major theme during the 91st Congress of 1969-1970, and appeared to become a fundamental trend that would go on well into the 1970's. It is constitutionally and politically difficult for the

Congress to take the initiative in foreign policy but it can demand that its consent be obtained.

The influence of the Congress in foreign affairs has fluctuated throughout the history of the Republic. Immediately after World War I, the Congress took the lead and held a predominant position over the President. The Senate, led by Henry Cabot Lodge, refused to approve the Versailles Peace Treaty and rejected the entry of the United States into the League of Nations, thereby rebuking President Wilson. The presidency did not recover from that defeat until well into the administration of President Roosevelt. He made executive agreements with other nations, in the advent of World War II, on lend-lease shipments of military equipment and moved into a preeminent position during the war itself as commander-in-chief of the armed forces.

The Congress regained some influence in the postwar period when the United States undertook many commitments abroad through mutual security treaties that required Senate assent and by pledging funds for the Marshall Plan and other economic assistance programs that required the approval of both the Senate and House. At the same time, however, the urgencies of the Cold War led President Truman to conduct much of his foreign policy through executive agreements or his authority as commander-in-chief. There were Congressional resolutions supporting Mr. Truman's move into the Korean War but the President never asked for the congressional declaration of war that many constitutional scholars and politicians thought was legally necessary for American forces to fight in Korea. Later, Presidents Eisenhower, Kennedy, and Johnson rarely sought Congressional approval, in the formal sense, of their decisions on the Middle East, Cuba, the Dominican Republic, or Vietnam.

President Johnson did ask for one show of Congressional support, the Tonkin Gulf Resolution of August, 1964. It turned out to be the high point of Presidential dominance in foreign policy. The resolution was drawn up in the White House and submitted to the Congress after two American destroyers were allegedly attacked during the night by North Vietnamese patrol boats in the waters off the coast of North Vietnam. President Johnson asked Congress to give him what amounted to a blank check to respond as he thought best in Southeast Asia. The resolution said: "The Congress approves and supports the determination of the President, as Commander in Chief, to take all necessary measures to repel any armed attack against the forces of the United States and to prevent further aggression." Mr. Johnson said later that he interpreted "all necessary measures" to mean that "the sky is the limit" on what he could do in Vietnam.

As the Vietnam venture turned sour, however, disenchantment set in, especially with Senator Fulbright. That was the proximate cause of the reversal of the long-term flow of authority from Capitol Hill to the White House. It led to the hearings before the Senate Foreign Relations Committee during the summer of 1967. One key witness, Undersecretary of State Nicholas de B. Katzenbach, contended that the President had full authority to conduct foreign affairs without restraint, except to make treaties. Moreover, he asserted that treaties were no longer important in making international agreements and that even the Congressional right to declare war had become outmoded in a day when "police action" and efforts to combat Communist-inspired "wars of national liberation" were the main conflicts.

But that view did not prevail, either in the Congress or in the subsequent administration of President Nixon. His Secretary of State, William P. Rogers, felt that Mr. Katzenbach's position was too aggressive and pledged to undertake full consultation with the Congress on major decisions of foreign policy. More important, the mood of the nation gave Senators considerable political leverage in demanding a voice on foreign policy. Many politically articulate Americans had come to believe in the late 1960's that the United States was overextended in its commitments abroad, that it was necessary to reallocate the nation's resources to solve the problems of urban decay, racial unrest, inadequate education, inflation, unemployment, and other domestic ills. Even deeper was the revival of a traditional current of isolation, of not having entangling alliances abroad, of not being the policeman of the world. While it was impossible for the United States to abdicate its position of leadership, there was a demand that America lessen its presence abroad and share with other nations the burden of maintaining the peace and providing for security. Senators in sympathy with that mood were able to use it effectively in curtailing the President's freedom to make decisions without Congressional assent.

Those attitudes led the Senate to adopt in June, 1969, a National Commitments resolution by a vote of 70–16. It was a turning point in the oscillation of influence between the Congress and the White House and sent power flowing back toward Capitol Hill. The resolution was not legally binding but it represented a political reality. The first draft was introduced by Senator Fulbright as a result of his committee's hearings in 1967. After two years of off-and-on debate, it was passed in this version:

Whereas accurate definition of the term "national commitment" in recent years has become obscured: Now, therefore, be it:

Resolved, that a national commitment for the purpose of this resolution means the use of the armed forces on foreign territory, or a promise to assist a foreign country, government, or people by the use of the armed forces or financial resources of the United States, either immediately or upon the happening of certain events, and

That it is the sense of the Senate that a national commitment by the United States results only from affirmative action taken by the Legislative and Executive Branches of the United States Government by means of a treaty, statute, or a concurrent resolution of both Houses of Congress specifically providing for such commitments.

The authority of the Congress in foreign affairs is rooted in one constitutional clause giving it the right to declare war and in another giving the Senate the right to render its advice and consent by a two-thirds vote on treaties proposed by the President. Equally important, the Congress must appropriate the funds the President needs to carry out his foreign policy. That gives the Congress, especially the House, where appropriation bills must originate, tremendous power in basic decisions on foreign policy. Since World War II, a great part of American diplomacy has been conducted through military expenditures and deployment of forces, military and economic assistance to other nations, and contributions to international organizations. There is little that the United States does in foreign policy that does not cost money—and that must come from the Congress.

Yet the Congress for many years was reluctant to exercise its power over the purse. It usually gave the President what he wanted, with the exception of foreign aid, which was steadily cut each year. Much of that reluctance could be attributed to the House of Representatives, whose members are attuned primarily to the local constituencies that they must face in an election every two years. Individual Representatives often lacked the interest in foreign affairs to spend the required time doing their homework and thus went along with the President's requests.

But when the American involvement in Southeast Asia started to be questioned extensively, the Congress began looking to its control of funds to influence policy. In 1969 and 1970, the Congress stipulated that no funds could be used to support American ground forces in Thailand, Cambodia, and Laos. Moreover, Senators Mark O. Hatfield, Republican of Oregon, and George S. McGovern, Democrat of South Dakota, asked the Senate to cut off funds for all American operations in Vietnam by the end of 1971. That effort failed but it signaled another warning to the President that henceforth the Congress would increasingly use its authority over appropriations to have a say in foreign policy. On the military side, there was a similar attitude toward appropriations in general. After years of giving the Pentagon almost everything it asked for, the Congress began to question seriously the need for ever-increasing military budgets and to cut them back. President Nixon was able to get only part of his proposed anti-ballistics missile (ABM) system, Safeguard, approved and that only by close votes.

One of the great traditions of parliamentary government is making executive officials answer to the legislature on matters both of high policy and daily action. Bringing a cabinet officer before the bar of legislative and public opinion to account for his stewardship can have considerable political impact. In Great Britain, cabinet ministers rise in the House of Commons to answer questions put to them by any member. The American version of public accountability is the congressional committee hearing.

Although a congressional committee, in the strict sense, calls hearings and invites witnesses to gather information about pending legislation, the practice has developed so that a committee can call a hearing for almost any reason it desires so long as the subject lies within its legislative jurisdiction. Members of the administration are invited to appear at those sessions to explain and defend their policies and decisions. The administration, however, may claim executive privilege for its officials to prevent them from testifying on the grounds that they are responsible to the President, as head of the executive branch, and are therefore not accountable to the Congress for their actions. As a rule, cabinet and sub-cabinet officers accept an invitation to testify. Not to do so usually produces a cry in the press that they are hiding something. White House officials, on the other hand, almost always decline on the ground that they are staff officers and not policy officers in the same sense as members of the cabinet. Even so, any administration takes a risk by exercising too much executive privilege. That became particularly true during the Nixon Administration after it became apparent that the President's Assistant for National Security Affairs, Dr. Kissinger, was closer to foreign policy decisions than was the Secretary of State, Mr. Rogers. In early 1971, Senator Stuart Symington, Democrat of Missouri, brought out into the open what all Washington had been gossiping about for a year and charged that Mr. Rogers had become a "laughing stock" because Dr. Kissinger had become the Secretary of State in all but name. Senator Fulbright immediately joined Senator Symington in the criticism, all of which grew largely out of the frustration the Senators felt when they could not get Dr. Kissinger to brief them on the administration's policies. Senator Fulbright later introduced legislation to restrict executive privilege, claiming that it was a custom and not a law. Along with other manifestations of a congressional resurgence in foreign policy, the Senate particularly seemed eager to question those officials at the heart of the decision-making process in a highly-centralized administration.

The principal committees that delve into foreign policy are the Senate Foreign Relations and the House Foreign Affairs Committees, the Senate and the House Armed Services Committees, and the Senate and the House Appropriations Committees. The Senate Commerce Committee and the House Interstate and Foreign Commerce Committee hold hearings when trade or other economic matters are concerned and other committees may dip into foreign affairs on peripheral issues.

Unfortunately, all too many of the hearings are in closed session because secret matters, or allegedly secret matters, are discussed. Thus the public is uninformed about what took place. Such sessions give Congressmen an opportunity to question the administration and administration officials are presumably more candid behind closed doors than they are in public. But administration officials are also able to bind the hands of the Congress by obtaining a promise that whatever was said will not be used in public. That, in effect, deprives the Congress of a valuable lever.

Other hearings, however, are open and, in the Senate, are covered both by the "pad-and-pencil" press and by television. The Senate Foreign Relations Committee held televised hearings in 1966 on the policy of the United States toward Communist China during which a scholar of Chinese affairs, A. Doak Barnett, then of Columbia University, suggested that American policy toward China should be "containment but not isolation." That simple but sweeping phrase caught on and helped to persuade the Congress, two administrations, and the public to adopt a more flexible attitude toward China and to abandon the rigid, antagonistic attitude of the 1950's and early 1960's. Similarly, hearings on Vietnam have been focal points for increasing Congressional dissent with successive administrations' policies in Vietnam and, historically, may be credited with having exerted a strong influence on turning that policy from intervention to disengagement.

In another form of Congressional hearing, witnesses testify in private but a transcript of their testimony is later issued with the sensitive secret material deleted. The most effective of those hearings in recent years was a series held by a subcommittee of the Senate Foreign Relations Committee headed by Senator Symington. The Symington subcommittee was established as a result of the National Commitments Resolution and was charged with investigating the entire range of American commitments abroad from the end of World War II. The subcommittee looked into treaty, executive, military, economic, and every other commitment made by the Congress, the President, and other American officials to nations from Korea around to Western Europe. It turned up several pledges that had been made secretly and without the consent of the Congress. All of the testimony was taken in private but transcripts of the hearings on each country, plus a summary review, were issued later.

There was a battle between the subcommittee staff and officials in the Departments of State and Defense and the Central Intelligence Agency over each transcript—indeed, over many paragraphs and sentences. But Senator Symington insisted that the executive branch be allowed to mark out only those items of extreme sensitivity. The published transcripts were documents that illuminated well the creeping commitment of American power abroad without Congressional assent in the last twenty-five years. The subcommittee's insistence on knowing a great deal more than successive administrations had told the Congress and its explicit criticisms of many commitments made clear to the incumbent Nixon Administration that new commitments would be subjected to careful scrutiny by the Senate and would not be approved unless Congressional thinking had been fully considered.

During the ascendancy of the executive branch in foreign

policy, the Congressional resolution was an instrument the President used to give the American public and governments of other nations the impression that he had the Congress behind him. With the pendulum swinging the other way, the Congressional resolution has become a device through which the Congress makes its wishes and, at times, its demands known to the President. During the rise to the peak of presidential power, the Tonkin Gulf resolution was passed. During the downslide, in 1970, it was repealed. Though those resolutions lack the force of law, they have the force of politics. They can be warnings to the President that unless Congressional advice is heeded, he may have trouble when appropriations time rolls around.

In the fall of 1969, the Senate used a "sense of the Senate" resolution to tell President Nixon that he should not make a firm commitment to the Japanese government to return the island of Okinawa to Japan without first obtaining the advice and consent of the Senate. The Senate approved the resolution by a vote of 63 to 14 just a few days before Prime Minister Eisaku Sato arrived in Washington to negotiate an agreement with President Nixon on the island's reversion. The joint communiqué announcing their agreement contained a pledge by both governments that it would become final only after appropriate legislative consultation. More important than the effect of the resolution on the Okinawa question was its strong and clear indication that the Senate was demanding to be heard even though a majority of Senators would probably have readily approved the Nixon-Sato agreement. Resolutions on foreign policy are ordinarily introduced by senior Senators who enjoy considerable prestige. They are debated at length before a vote is taken. In contrast, the resolution on Okinawa was introduced by Senator Harry F. Byrd, Jr., Democrat of Virginia, who was the junior member of the Senate Foreign Relations Committee on the majority side. It was debated for only an hour and approved with only desultory opposition, indicating the mood of the Senate in reasserting its prerogatives on foreign policy. That resolution, plus the general mood of the Senate, persuaded the President to put the reversion of Okinawa in the form of a treaty rather than an executive agreement. The treaty was then passed by the Senate in the fall of 1971 with only minimum opposition.

The Constitution prescribes that the President shall appoint his ambassadors with the advice and consent of the Senate. The nominee usually appears at a hearing of the Foreign Relations Committee to answer questions. The committee then votes to send the nomination to the floor for approval. For the most part, the process is routine because the Senate operates on the assumption that the President ought to be able to pick his own ambassadors unless he makes an outrageous selection or chooses someone who is patently offensive to a Senator. But that precedent may be changing. During President Nixon's Administration, the nominations of a conservative professor to be ambassador to Morocco and an oilman to be ambassador to Venezuela were quietly withdrawn when some Senators expressed objections on grounds of ideological differences or alleged conflict of interest.

Lastly, the Congress is as much a forum as a legislature. For all its faults and idiosyncracies, the Congress of the United States is truly a focal point of national debate. On the floor of either house can be heard reasoned, well-informed debate and impassioned, muddled discussion of foreign policy ranging from questions of defense against nuclear attack to the administration's plans for opening up markets in Western Europe for American fried chicken. Some of those debates are reported in the press but unhappily for the American people, not enough. They are known to the executive branch, however, through the Congressional Record that is printed each day or through the grapevine that moves information through Washington. A particular speech or a given debate may not make much of a dent in a specific question at hand, although that is possible. But individual Senators and Representatives who have done their homework, have solid constituencies behind them, and speak for strong vested interests can have a major impact. Moreover, all of the words cumulatively constitute a flood with which an administration must move since it cannot be dammed up.

8

The Arm of
the Law

AT FIRST GLANCE, the federal courts and the quasi-judicial federal regulatory agencies might seem remote from the making of foreign policy. But the Constitution gives the courts a basic legal role. Beyond that, they have influenced or determined decisions in foreign affairs by making legal precedent as the United States has become ever more engaged in a myriad of relationships with other nations. The functions of the courts and the regulatory agencies, in turn, have been affected by the actions of other nations toward the United States. Few of those connections have been dramatic but many have caused changes in the lives of Americans and in the overall relations of the United States with another country.

The Constitution, in Article VI, says that "all treaties made, or which shall be made, under the authority of the United States, shall be the supreme law of the land." Thus, the making of a treaty brings in all three branches of government—the President as proposer and final signer, the Senate as approver by two-thirds major, and the judiciary as interpreter and legal guardian. The Constitution gives federal courts jurisdiction over cases arising from treaties, those concerning foreign ambassadors in the United States, and those concerning admiralty and maritime matters. The

Supreme Court itself has original jurisdiction in cases involving ambassadors; in others it has appellate jurisdiction.

The link between the courts and foreign policy was shown vividly, if inconclusively, in a controversy over a Status of Forces Agreement between the United States and the Republic of Korea. The case centered on a young American soldier who was tried and convicted in a Korean court for strangling a Korean prostitute in 1968.

The Status of Forces Agreement, which went into effect in February, 1967, is a lengthy document that prescribes in detail the legal status under which American military forces are posted in Korea. The agreement, known in government jargon as SOFA, is similar to those the United States has with members of the North Atlantic Treaty Organization, Japan, and most other nations in which American troops are stationed.

The SOFAs include a multitude of provisions on customs duties, taxation, driver's licenses, and post exchange privileges. The most important articles define criminal jurisdiction over American military personnel who commit crimes in a foreign land. The SOFAs vary slightly from country to country but usually provide that an American who commits a crime while on duty, or on his base, will be tried in an American military court. An American soldier who commits a crime while off duty, or off his base, is subject to arrest and trial in a court of the host nation.

American lawyers, both military and civilian, have long disagreed about the legality of the criminal jurisdiction provisions of the SOFAs. Some contend that an American soldier cannot be deprived of the fundamental legal rights of an American citizen no matter where he is serving. They argue that the soldier is subject to the United States Universal Code of Military Justice and civil law while he is in the armed services. They further maintain that the soldier is overseas because he was ordered there by his superiors and not by choice, as a tourist might be. Therefore, they claim, the United States government is responsible for preserving his constitutional rights.

Other legal experts contend, on the other hand, that international law and custom dictate that a sovereign nation has the right to exercise criminal jurisdiction over anyone who commits a crime within its territory. American diplomats, moreover, argue that the national pride of people in most nations demands that their authorities retain control over law enforcement.

Most of the SOFAs, therefore, are a compromise. They provide that the standards of a trial of an American soldier be comparable with those in the United States. But the laws and specific legal procedures of the host nation prevail.

On the night of February 28, 1968, Specialist Four H. K. Smallwood, of Keith, Kentucky, left his barracks in the 19th General Support Group in Seoul to go into a honky-tonk section of the city. He returned to his barracks past the curfew hour, which was noted in a complaint written up by the military police when he passed through the gate.

The next day, the body of a Korean prostitute was found in the charred ruins of her house. Korean authorities, after a preliminary investigation, charged that Smallwood had murdered the girl and set her house afire to cover the crime. American military authorities conducted a separate investigation but concluded that the evidence was not enough to arrest Smallwood. The Koreans insisted, however, on taking jurisdiction of the case under the SOFA. The Americans agreed.

While in an Army stockade awaiting trial, Smallwood got the help of several young Army lawyers who believed that he would not get a fair trial in a Korean court. They persuaded an attorney in Washington to petition for a writ of habeas corpus on the United States District Court in Washington. The attorney, using information supplied by the young Army lawyers in Korea, listed eleven shortcomings of the Korean legal system. He asked that Smallwood be brought to the United States and be given a hearing to prove that he could not have a fair trial in Korea. He further asked that Smallwood not be turned over to the Korean authorities for trial.

The judge, however, denied the petition. In his finding, he said: "Realistically, the question resolves itself into a balancing of the national interest justifying the stationing of troops abroad against the possibility of any deprivation of constitutionally protected rights at the hands of foreign local law which does not conform to American standards."

"It is the determination of this court," the judge ruled, "that the national interest outweighs any other considerations. To argue that under the applicable rule of international law, visiting forces retain jurisdiction is to close one's eyes to the historical fact that this matter is no longer left up to the implications of law but is carefully expressed in agreements which are explicit qualifications of consent to station visiting forces."

Smallwood's attorney went immediately to the Court of Appeals and was successful in obtaining a restraining order. It allowed the Army to surrender Smallwood to the Koreans for trial but ordered that he not be released to Korean custody until the appellate court in Washington had decided whether his plea should be heard in a United States Federal Court.

In July, 1968, Smallwood was tried, convicted, and sentenced to fifteen years in prison by the Korean court. But he was kept in the Army stockade while his attorney and the United States Attorney, representing the Army and opposing Smallwood's plea, prepared briefs to argue before the Court of Appeals. Smallwood also appealed the conviction to the Korean Court of Appeals.

By this time, the Smallwood case had caused considerable turmoil within the American and Korean governments and had generated some friction between officials of the two governments. The case hit at a particularly sensitive time, shortly after the crisis caused by a North Korean attempt to assassinate President Park Chung Hee of South Korea and North Korea's seizure of the American intelligence ship *Pueblo* in January, 1968. The United States, deeply engaged in Southeast Asia, wanted to negotiate with the North Koreans; the South Koreans, fearing that a show of weakness would only encourage more North Korean hostility, wanted to retaliate against North Korea. That disagreement in policy led to a number of testy exchanges between American and Korean officials.

Thus, the South Koreans, already upset over earlier differences, were further angered by what they considered unfounded criticism of their legal system. They also feared that the SOFA might be renegotiated or abrogated, which would have been a slicing cut to their national pride. American military leaders and diplomats spent much time during those months assuring Korean leaders that the views expressed by Smallwood and his lawyers did not represent the official view of the United States toward the SOFA. The Americans were anxious to prevent the Smallwood case from hurting their working relationships with the Koreans on political and military matters.

In Washington, Smallwood's attorney, in his brief to the Court of Appeals, not only challenged the capacity of the Korean court to give him a fair trial but also questioned the legality of the SOFA itself. The attorney contended that the SOFA was illegal because it had not been approved by the Senate in the form of a treaty, as other SOFAs had, but had been arranged by presidential executive agreement. Smallwood's attorney further argued that the SOFA was unconstitutional because it deprived Smallwood of his basic rights as an American citizen. He quoted Justice Hugo L. Black of the Supreme Court in an earlier decision in which the Justice wrote:

The concept that the Bill of Rights and other constitutional protections against arbitrary government are inoperative when they become inconvenient or when expendiency dictates otherwise is a very dangerous doctrine and if allowed to flourish would destroy the benefit of a written constitution and undermine the basis of our government.

If our foreign commitments become of such a nature that the government can no longer satisfactorily operate within the bounds laid down by the Constitution, that instrument can be amended by the method it prescribes. But we have no authority, or inclination, to read exceptions into it which are not there.

Officials in the Pentagon and the State Department sensed that the Smallwood case might go all the way to the Supreme Court and realized that, if the Court ruled in favor of Smallwood, it would set a precedent endangering all of the SOFAs. The legal question would not come up in the SOFA with NATO since it had been approved as a treaty by the Senate. The SOFA with Japan, although not a treaty, had been ruled legal by the Supreme Court in a test case on the grounds that the Senate was aware that it would be added to another treaty with Japan. But the legality of the rest would be open to question and the constitutional validity of all might be destroyed on the basis of Justice Black's opinion.

After many consultations in Washington and a stream of cables between Washington and the American military and diplomatic establishment in Seoul, American officials decided to persuade the Koreans to drop the charges against Smallwood when his case came up in the Korean Court of Appeals. There were no formal representations made to the Korean government. But an American general in Seoul sought out senior officials of the Korean Ministry of Justice at a cocktail party and told them that he thought the case would go to the Supreme Court. He said he wasn't sure that the United States Attorney would win the case, and if he lost that would jeopardize the SOFA. He hinted that publicity for the Korean courts during the American court proceedings would be bad and explained that an adverse decision would affect other SOFAs with other American allies.

The Korean officials quickly saw the point. They quietly passed the word to the judge in the Korean Court of Appeals, who acquitted Smallwood and set him free. The judge said that he was 99 percent sure that Smallwood had committed the murder with which he was charged but that he was willing to give him one percent of the doubt. With the case over in the Korean courts, it became moot in the United States Court of Appeals. The case thus never reached the Supreme Court and the questions of legality and constitutionality of the SOFA were left undecided. But the entire episode had made its mark on American foreign policy.

Another arm of the law, and perhaps the most obscure arm of the United States government, is the collection of federal regulatory agencies in Washington. Among them are the Securities and Exchange Commission, which sets rules for issuing, buying, and selling corporate stocks; the Civil Aeronautics Board, which regulates the routes and fares of air transport; the Federal Communications Commission, which governs the use of radio and television airways; the Federal Power Commission, which regulates the gas and electric power industries; and the Federal Trade Commission, which is responsible for seeing that commerce is conducted fairly. They, and others, were established by the Congress and are responsible to the Congress for overseeing the operations of many vital portions of the nation's economy. The President appoints members of the commissions and recommends, through the Office of Management and Budget, their annual budgets. But the regulatory agencies' functions are quasi-judicial. They conduct hearings on proposals and disputes before examiners who act in the manner of judges and the decisions of a commission have the effect of law. The courts, however, have the final decision on disputes that a commission and an industry cannot settle.

The regulatory agencies, which are primarily concerned with the internal economy of the nation, get into foreign relations in varying degrees. Several have bureaus headed by a senior official who is responsible for looking after the agency's international affairs, usually in conjunction with the Department of State. Most of their foreign problems are routine but once in a while the foreign policy of the United States comes into play.

A fairly common incident was a Securities and Exchange Commission investigation into an alleged $100 million fraud of American and Canadian investors by a ring that operated in the United States, Canada, Panama, the Bahamas, Britain, and Western Europe. In 1968, the SEC charged in an Illinois court that the conspirators, led by one Michael M. Rush, a Canadian, had victimized more than five hundred persons by persuading shareholders in dormant American and Canadian companies to exchange their shares for stock in fictitious companies. Transfer fees and certain American taxes were collected from the investors. The ring, which had its offices in Panama and the Bahamas, also sold shares in worthless corporations supposedly active in mining, coffee, real estate, and other ventures in Panama, South America, Europe, and Africa.

The SEC began investigating the ring after it received complaints from suspicious investors. The commission then brought the Internal Revenue Service, the Treasury, the Department of State, and the Federal Bureau of Investigation into the inquiry. Working through the State Department, the SEC investigators gathered information from the governments of Canada, Panama, Britain, and others. When they thought they had enough evidence, they went into the Illinois court since several of the allegedly defrauded investors lived in that state. In February, 1969, the SEC obtained a permanent injunction against Rush and his colleagues and in May had them indicted on sixty-one counts of fraud and violation of the securities laws. The defendants were not brought to trial since they had fled but the international action broke up their ring.

A regulatory agency much more involved in foreign affairs than the SEC is the Civil Aeronautics Board. The CAB receives applications, holds hearings, and grants permits to foreign airlines that wish to fly into the United States. Overall agreements on landing rights are negotiated with other nations by the State Department with the help of CAB's Bureau of International Aviation. Conversely, the CAB receives applications, holds hearings, and grants American carriers the right to fly routes abroad. Those must be approved by the government of the country in which the American carriers wish to land. The State Department negotiates those rights, again with the advice of the CAB's Bureau of International Aviation.

An illuminating case of the conflicting interplay between foreign policy and domestic politics and economics was the Transpacific route controversy of 1968–1969. On the American side, it involved the CAB, Presidents Johnson and Nixon and their White House staffs, the Department of State, and the Department of Transportation, plus about twenty American airlines. On the foreign side were the governments of Japan, Nationalist China, Australia, and New Zealand, plus the national airlines of each nation.

For several years in the mid-1960's, various American airlines had applied to the CAB for new routes across the Pacific to the Orient and Australia. In 1967, the CAB consolidated all of the applications and began hearings in which a representative of each airline appeared before an examiner and contended that his airline should receive one or more of the lucrative new routes.

After months of hearings and volumes of testimony, the examiner recommended to the CAB a vast pattern of new routes and airlines to fly them. The board, however, voted to change several in response to persuasion members had received from airline representatives and sent the awarded international routes to President Johnson for his approval. The CAB has the final say on domestic routes but the President, with his constitutional authority in foreign policy, must approve all overseas routes.

Among the awards of international routes was one for American Airlines from the mainland of the United States through Hawaii to Japan and back. The Japanese government, informed of this by the State Department, protested vigorously. The United States already had two airlines flying to Japan, the Japanese said, and a third was not wanted. The Japanese government, which controls Japan Air Lines, the national flag carrier, did not want more competition for JAL. The State Department, on receipt of the Japanese protest, recommended to the White House that the route awarded to American Airlines be deleted. Officials in the State Department said that allowing the award to go through would aggravate other negotiations with the Japanese over the return of Okinawa, trade, and foreign investment. The President accepted the State Department recommendation and disapproved the route for American Airlines.

But President Johnson's decision, which came at the tag end of his administration, opened the door for a battle royal. In the route system devised by the CAB, the domestic routes and the international routes were intended to fit together in an integrated pattern. To revise one route meant revising the entire pattern. President Johnson's aides tried to patch a revision together but before that could be completed, President Nixon came to office.

President Nixon's aides took one look at the problem, decided that the pattern had to be entirely rearranged, and threw it back to the CAB. But the board didn't agree with the instructions given it by the White House and there followed six months of bureaucratic infighting over who was to determine the revised route structure, lobbying by airlines representatives, charges by Republicans that President Johnson had favored certain airlines, countercharges by Democrats that President Nixon favored others, and even attempts to get the courts into the fight. After much bargaining and compromising and with no one very happy, the dispute was settled in mid-1969. There was only a modest increase in service from the United States to Japan and that by the two carriers, Pan American and Northwest Orient, already flying there. American Airlines and the other carriers who had applied for routes either got nothing or were awarded less profitable routes through Hawaii to the South Pacific. That was the outcome of the turmoil caused by one foreign government having objected to one segment of the vast new pattern that had been proposed.

9

A Potpourri
of Pressures

BEYOND the official foreign affairs community in Washington is what might be called the greater national foreign affairs community. It comprises lobbyists for business, labor, and foreign governments; the academic world and research organizations known as "think tanks"; the foundations, such as the Ford Foundation and the Rockefeller Foundation that finance studies and projects related to foreign affairs; civic organizations; the news media; and the American public itself.

The various elements in that diffuse community exert their influence on the official foreign policy community formally and informally through consultations, meetings, publishing, articles in the press and programs on television, and by the mobilization of public opinion. At times the pressures are directed at specific policies; at other times, they are concerned more with the longer trend and directions of foreign policy. In all of this, the press has far less influence than most people think, whether they are giving it credit or accusing it of evil. The primary function of the press is to provide a channel of communications among the diverse elements of the foreign policy community and especially between the people and their leaders. Conversely, the public is much more powerful than is widely believed in a day when the institutions and processes of democracy are being carefully scrutinized, skeptically questioned, and frequently held up to scorn.

Lobbyists for foreign governments or private industry, labor, and trade associations are paid professional public relations practitioners or lawyers in Washington and, to a lesser extent, New York. Their objective is to influence the decisions made by the United States government in favor of the governments or the private interests they represent. Anyone representing a foreign government or private interest must register as a foreign agent with the Department of Justice. But most of them operate well out of the public eye. They try to present persuasive arguments on behalf of their clients to officials in the White House, the Department of State, the Agency for International Development, and other agencies involved in a particular question. Lobbyists are particularly active on Capitol Hill, where they present their contentions to Congressmen and their staffs on pending legislation such as bills on foreign aid or trade. The lobbyists are often in touch with the press in hopes of having articles printed that favor their clients. They are often wasting their time since news reporters are not interested in what they refer to as "puff pieces." Moreover, a sophisticated official or Congressman sees through the effort rather quickly and is far more impressed by the merits of a position than by stories appearing in the newspapers. On the other hand, a news story can be helpful to the lobbyist in getting the attention of officials or Congressional staffs when an issue has been shunted aside or ignored.

Among the more active lobbies in Washington in recent years have been those representing Israel, Nationalist China, and Japan. The Israelis, working through American organizations such as B'nai B'rith, have worked to maintain the long-standing but unwritten American commitment to the preservation of Israel in the face of the continuing threat from its Arab neighbors. Lobbyists specifically have tried to persuade the American government to increase its shipments of arms and its economic aid to Israel.

The Nationalist Chinese have worked through paid public relations firms and through what was known as the China Lobby, a group of prominent Americans who were sympathetic to the government of President Chiang Kai-shek on Taiwan. Lobbyists for the Nationalist Chinese have tried to persuade successive administrations, the Congress, bureaucrats, and the press that the United States treaty commitment to their client should be kept strong and that no accommodation with Communist China should be sought. The old China Lobby has become inactive in recent years and has been replaced by a group of scholars, businessmen, and labor leaders who contend, much to the consternation of the Nationalist Chinese, that an accommodation with Communist China would be in the best national interests of the United States.

The lobby for the Japanese is a conglomeration of several lawyers and a battery of public relations men who focus mainly on trade problems. The United States-Japan Trade Council in Washington, which is registered as an agent of the Japanese government, publishes pamphlets and issues press releases to promote Japanese exports to the United States. Officials of the Council are particularly active in trying to ward off legislation or rulings in the executive branch that the Japanese consider to be protectionist and discriminatory against Japanese trade.

Lobbyists for domestic interests operate in much the same way, although they are less restricted by law and by protocol. Nearly every industry and many corporations, plus the labor unions, have representatives in Washington to insure that their points of view are made known to policy-makers, both publicly and privately. In 1970, they lined up and did battle over a trade bill that, had it passed, would have severely restricted the importation of textiles, shoes, and other products by setting quotas. Advocates of the bill included lobbyists from the textile, shoe, steel, chemical, and oil industries, plus dozens of smaller industries such as mink raisers. On the other side were lobbyists for agriculture, retail merchants, international corporations, and most local chambers of commerce.

But it was the labor lobby that almost tipped the balance in favor of the protectionists.

Representing the protectionists were Thomas F. Shannon of the American Footwear Manufacturers Association and Robert C. Jackson of the American Textile Manufacturers Institute, both of whom spent most of the year talking to people on Capitol Hill. The free-traders were less well organized but Claude J. Desautels of the American Soybean Association, whose member firms export about $1 billion worth of crops a year and feared retaliation from foreign nations, worked hard against the bill. In addition, the Emergency Committee for American Trade, which was supported by international corporations such as Xerox, Honeywell, and International Business Machines, was represented by Robert L. McNeil, who had been a Deputy Assistant Secretary of Commerce in the Johnson Administration. Perhaps the most active of them all, however, was Evelyn Dubrow, the lobbyist for the International Ladies Garment Workers Union. She estimated that during the last six months of 1970, she visited 350 of the 435 Congressmen and 50 of the 100 Senators to plead her case. She was given credit on Capitol Hill for swinging enough votes to have the bill passed by the House and to be voted out of the Senate Finance Committee. The bill died, however, when time ran out and the 91st Congress came to an end.

Academicians, mostly social scientists, have both immediate and longer term influence on foreign policy. The influence of the scholar working in a research "think tank" may be more direct than that of his colleague in the university as many work on projects funded by the government. Some research organizations, such as the Institute for Defense Analysis, are closely tied to the Pentagon. Others, such as the RAND Corporation in California and the Hudson Institute in New York, carry on projects under contract. Still others, such as the Brookings Institution in Washington, eschew government work. But the scholars there are available to government officials for consultation. The counsel of those scholars and their associates in the universities is often sought by officials in the Department of State, the Central Intelligence

Agency, and the White House on specific questions. An official involved in China policy, for instance, may pick up the telephone to call Allen Whiting, a political scientist who specializes in Chinese affairs at the University of Michigan, or Doak Barnett, a China hand at the Brookings Institution. The questions asked are more likely to be along the lines of "What do you think Chou En-lai meant when he said such-and-such?" rather than "What do you think the government should do about such-and-such incident?"

The longer range influence of scholars on foreign policy comes from the books and articles they write, which affect the thinking of policy-makers, and through their lecturing and teaching, which help to form the minds of the young people from whom will come the next generation of political leaders and policy-makers.

Academicians, however, do advise on policy in a more formal sense. The Department of State has advisory committees composed of scholars who are asked for advice on what they think United States policy should be. Edwin O. Reischauer, a leading student of Japanese history at Harvard, then Ambassador to Japan in the Kennedy and early Johnson Administrations, and after that University Professor at Harvard, is frequently consulted on American policy toward Japan. The Department of State and the National Security Council staff also commission research papers to done by specialists in the academic world on both their analysis of a particular question and their recommendations to resolve it. That gives the foreign policy official a view of the issue that is supposedly free of bureaucratic or political bias.

The academic world became a source of political appointments to high office and ambassadorships beginning with the Kennedy Administration and continuing through the Nixon Administration. Particularly notable was President Kennedy's appointment of McGeorge Bundy, from Harvard, as his Assistant for National Security Affairs in the White House. When Mr. Bundy left, he was replaced by Walt W. Rostow from the Massachusetts Institute of Technology, who was named by President Johnson. In turn, President Nixon appointed Dr. Henry A. Kissinger from Harvard and made him into the single most important official in the foreign policy community of the Nixon Administration.

With the rise in dissent over American policy in Southeast Asia, some scholars became activists in trying to mold foreign policy. They helped to organize demonstrations, rallies, and ad hoc committees of protest, wrote highly polemic tracts, and lectured widely to publicize their political positions. Among the most militant were Professor Staughton Lynd, of Yale, who traveled to Hanoi both to seek a way toward peace and to dramatize his opposition to the war in Vietnam. Professor Noam Chomsky, of MIT, who is a specialist in linguistics, visited several countries in Southeast Asia and returned to write inflammatory criticism of American action there.

Several scholarly professional associations became active in efforts to influence policy, largely through the demands of younger and often left-leaning scholars. That touched off a great debate within the associations, with the majority of the older scholars contending that their associations should devote themselves to the problems of the professions such as improving the quality of scholarship, obtaining better working conditions for scholars, and increasing the availability of research funds. The younger scholars argued that this was not enough, that they as individuals and the professional associations should seek to have a political impact on policy.

Perhaps less obtrusive contributions to foreign policy are made by private foreign affairs associations. The grandfather of those civic organizations is the Council on Foreign Relations in New York City. Its members include prominent businessmen, professional men, labor leaders, scholars, and a sprinkling of government officials and journalists. They seek to educate themselves by having statesmen, senior government officials, and specialists from the United States and other nations present lectures or meet with them in informal, off-the-record discussions. The Council publishes the prestigious, if somewhat dull, quarterly called *Foreign Affairs*. The Council further commissions books for the enlightenment of both specialists in foreign affairs and the public. A series on various aspects of United States policy toward China, published in the late 1960's, was a singularly useful effort. The Council makes another contribution by offering fellowships each year to journalists, government and military officers, and scholars that give them several months or a year away from their regular work to read, research, write, and generally to think and refresh themselves on their areas of specialization. The recipients are expected to return to their regular jobs better prepared to contribute toward American thinking and decisions on foreign policy.

Other foreign affairs organizations across the nation carry on much the same work, though perhaps in not so elaborate a fashion as the New York Council. Some have struck off in other directions. The Philadelphia Council of World Affairs presents public lectures in which specialists from government, the universities, business, and the news media discuss their ideas or report on their research and experience. The Chicago Council on Foreign Relations, besides having an extensive lecture series, arranges panel discussions and seminars for high-school students and teachers in the greater Chicago area. That council believes that citizens must be reached at the high-school level if they are to have a genuine interest in and understanding of foreign nations and American relations with them.

A forum in which members of the official and unofficial foreign affairs communities meet to exchange ideas and information is the American Assembly, an adjunct of Columbia University. The Assembly regularly invites several score of men and women interested in a given subject to Arden House, the estate overlooking the Hudson River that was once the home of former Governor Averell Harriman's family. For three or four days, they discuss United States relations with Latin America, or with Japan, or they dig into the problems of disarmament or population. The assembly hears speakers, discusses papers prepared by specialists, writes a general report, and collects the papers and report into a book that is distributed to a wider audience. Such meetings are especially useful in making officials concerned with policy aware of the thinking of a representative and informed segment of the unofficial community.

The most pervasive conveyors of information pertaining to foreign affairs are the nation's news media. They provide communications within the greater national foreign affairs community, between the official and unofficial elements of it, and between the decision-makers and the public. The press is, curiously, a channel of communications even within the official foreign policy community in Washington, which is so large and dispersed that official communications are often slow and ineffective. During preparations for the charter meeting of the Asian Development Bank in Bangkok in 1965, a routine message from the Soviet Union was received in the office of the Agency for International Development that was responsible for handling the United States participation. The message said that the Soviet Union, which had been invited to join the bank, would send an observer. That was the first expression of interest by the Soviet Union in joint economic aid to Southeast Asia and it had important political implications. A reporter making a routine check about preparations for the forthcoming meeting was told of the message and wrote a story about it. The article, which appeared on a Saturday morning, triggered a telephone call from then Secretary of State Dean Rusk to the AID office to find out what was going on. There was nothing secret about the Russian message but a memo informing the Secretary of its contents had not yet reached his desk—three floors above the AID office.

Yet, one of the great myths of American society is "the power of the press." That expression implies that the press has the authority to move events. But the press has no power. It cannot make a decision nor can it execute a policy. What the press does have, in the making of foreign policy or any other governmental policy, is influence. It is not a semantic quibble to draw the subtle but clear distinction between influence and power. Power means the authority to decide and to act. Influence means the capacity to inform and to persuade. The press has influence because it gathers, selects, and disseminates information. Correspondents in Washington, the United Nations, and foreign capitals around the world learn as much about the events and trends of international relations as they can. But then a critical process of selection sets in. The reporter allocates his time and attention to a limited number of topics. After he covers a story, he selects the facts and interpretations he thinks most significant, cutting out anywhere from 20 to 80 percent of what he knows because there is not space in the paper or time on the air to spill it all out. His editor enters the selective process by deciding what to print, how much, and where. Thus, the reader or viewer is given an intensely capsulized version of the information gathered by the reporter at the other end of the line. It is in that selective process that the press has its greatest influence—by determining what it will pass on to the readers and viewers. Editorials may try to persuade the readers to a particular point of view, but most newsmen would agree that editorials do not have the impact on the public that the selection of news has.

From then on, the readers and viewers decide for themselves what they will do with the information—and there is nothing the press can do about that. A newspaper can say what it thinks ought to be done in its editorial pages, or a television commentator may articulate his praise or criticism of what has been done. But the chasm between the capacity to persuade and the authority to decide cannot be spanned.

10

The Power of the People

ON THE EVENING of March 31, 1968, President Lyndon Baines Johnson addressed the nation on television to defend his policy on Vietnam and to announce that "I am taking the first step to deescalate the conflict." He said that he had ordered the bombing of major portions of North Vietnam to cease and urged the North Vietnamese to respond by agreeing to negotiations. He continued for some minutes in a philosophic vein, noting that "I have concluded that I should not permit the presidency to become involved in the partisan divisions that are developing in this political year." The President then stunned the nation by saying: "Accordingly, I shall not seek, and I will not accept, the nomination of my party for another term as your President."

In the best Johnsonian fashion, the President had achieved almost complete surprise. A few political observers in Washington had speculated over the year before that the President would not stand for reelection. But there was practically no one who put much credence in the thought. Lyndon Johnson, so the conventional widsom held, liked being President too much. But after the dust from his bombshell had blown away, it became increasingly clear that Mr. Johnson's decision was both logical and almost inevitable. He was a proud man who did not wish to risk defeat at the polls in the election coming up that November. He was also a shrewd, keenly attuned politician who had sensed that he had lost largely over his policy in Vietnam that intangible mandate of the people that allows a President to govern. Mr. Johnson, therefore, abdicated before he was thrown out of office by the voters. He came as close, in effect, to being forced out of office as the American political system allows without going through the wrenching process of impeachment.

Among the myths of American society, held by many officials and private citizens alike, is that the public has little to say in the making of the nation's foreign policy. It is widely believed that decisions on foreign policy, whether in the broad pronouncements that set a fundamental course or in the trivia of day-to-day execution, are the province of a small, elite group of specialists in Washington. But that is only partly true. By and large, the voters cannot have much say on specific, routine decisions since they are made out of the public eye and are too numerous, or insignificant, for public discussion. In the American form of government, the people have delegated much of that to their elected officials and indirectly to their appointed officers in the bureaucracy. But the people most assuredly have retained to themselves the constitutional power to alter the direction of foreign policy by dismissing those representatives and officials who pursue an unacceptable policy. That is perhaps an old-fashioned thought in a day when the foundations of democratic institutions and processes are being questioned and often held up to ridicule. But careful scrutiny suggests that the concept of the power of the people is still very much alive and valid.

Moreover, there have been instances in which the public has had a direct impact on a specific major decision. Immediately after President Nixon ordered American troops into Cambodia in the spring of 1970, waves of protest reached Washington from students, businessmen, professional men, workers, and just plain people. The protest was so striking that the President, even though his objectives were limited to begin with, was forced to modify his policy, to set a deadline for withdrawal of the troops from Cambodia, and to impose restraints on similar incursions in the future. Further, the Congress responded to the protest by voting to forbid the expenditure of funds for American ground forces in Cambodia and Laos. Thus, when an attempt to disrupt North Vietnamese supply lines in southern Laos was planned in early 1971, it was South Vietnamese and not Americans who went in as foot soldiers.

There was a day, before World War II, when the majority of the American people were perhaps not much concerned with foreign policy. It was confined then to everyday commerce between nations and did not involve national security, worldwide commitments, and matters of life and death to the degree that it did in the postwar era. In the period of Cold War and occasional hot wars that marked the next twenty-five years, the interest of the public in foreign affairs increased as pocketbooks were lightened by greater taxation and as sons went off to fight in wars beyond the seas. Even so, there was a tendency to leave the conduct of foreign affairs to the President, a relatively small number of advisers and bureaucrats, and a few interested Congressmen. That gave rise to an elitist psychology in the Department of State and the other elements of the foreign affairs bureaucracy. The belief there was that the American people were uninformed, uninterested, and incapable of knowing what the national interest was in foreign affairs. Many officials acquired a "leave-it-to-us" attitude that bordered on contempt for the electorate and its representatives in the Congress. They thought, perhaps subconsciously, that only they had the ability, the knowledge, and the judgment to know what is best for America. In contrast, bureaucrats dealing with domestic affairs instinctively knew that they must forever keep an eye on public and Congressional opinion. To fail to do so was to court political disaster.

The 1970's, however, are not the 1940's. In the late 1960's an increasing number of young adults began to demand that the people have a bigger voice in the making of all public policy, foreign and otherwise. In that, they appeared to have the sympathetic and often active support of a growing number of older citizens, despite the nationwide turning of attention to the domestic problems of racial strife, urban rot, environmental pollution, cancerous inflation, poverty, inadequate education, and a long list of other social ills. The dissent over the war in Vietnam spread from that issue to dissent over the elitist attitude and the secrecy surrounding decisions in foreign policy. The anti-war demonstrations and civil disturbances were but the most obvious manifestation of the change. More and more people wrote to their Congressmen, organized themselves into lobbies with their neighbors or with citizens of like mind or profession, wrote letters to editors, and found other ways to attract the attention of the news media. The formation of a new public-interest lobby called Common Cause in 1970 was based on the belief that thousands of ordinary citizens were dissatisfied with the institutions and processes of government, including those concerned with foreign policy. It set out to mobilize citizens to change both policies and processes. The reassertion of constitutional prerogatives by the Congress in the field of foreign policy in the late 1960's and early 1970's was stimulated, in part, by the realization that the voters back home were unhappy with the way the foreign affairs of their nation were being run.

Of all the lessons that might come out of the American experience in Vietnam, perhaps the most fundamental is that no American foreign policy can be successful without the implicit approval and understanding of the American people. That would seem to be obvious. But the history of the American involvement in Vietnam, dating back to 1954 or even to 1945, showed that administration after administration took the United States deeper and deeper into that quagmire without first obtaining the commitment from the American people that is prerequisite to making commitments to other people. When the American people ultimately became aware that they had been backed into Vietnam, they rebelled and the policy backfired. In particular, President Johnson was reluctant to justify candidly his reasons for more and more troops, more and more money, and more and more of a commitment to a dubious cause. Unhappily, his administration was caught in more misleading statements and outright lies than anyone cared to count. Consequently, a government that never enjoyed much public support for the Vietnam affair lost what little it had. In the end, the American people turned their President out of office.

Yet there was a serious question as to whether the lesson was learned by the subsequent administration and especially by the bureaucrats who make so much of the nation's foreign policy. President Nixon and his public relations advisers came to office with many protestations of an "open administration." The Department of State from time to time made efforts to explain various aspects of foreign policy to the public through speeches by senior officials, seminars by middle-ranking officers, publication of position papers, and a myriad of other public relations activities. But a poll in early 1971 showed that, on the Vietnam issue at least, a majority of the people believed that the Nixon Administration was not leveling with them. It also seemed clear that if the public did not trust the government on one major issue, it was not likely to trust it on others. And when a critical moment came, the public was not likely to support its government unless it could see that the administration's policy directly served the national interest or provided for the national security as they—and not the administration —saw it.

The trouble is, the citizen may ask himself, what can I do about all of this? It takes all of my time and energies just to live and work in this complex modern world. How can I be expected to educate myself on foreign policy and to take even a small part in influencing those decisions, especially when there are so many domestic ills around me that need to be cured.

As with most questions of public policy, there is no single or easy answer. But one thought might be offered. John Philpot Curran, in a speech in 1790 on the right of election of the Lord Mayor of Dublin, said: "The condition upon which God hath given liberty to man is eternal vigilance; which condition if he break, servitude is at once the consequence of his crime, and the punishment of his guilt." Perhaps the only answer is, then, a paraphrase of Curran: The citizen must be vigilant or else pay the consequences of his neglect. The citizen must concern himself, at least on the critical issues, with what his government does, or suffer from the mistakes and misjudgments his government makes. The citizen, through his representatives in the Congress, through the press, and through organizations concerned with foreign policy, can make known to his government that which he will accept and support and that which he won't. Singly, such actions make small dents. Collectively and accumulatively, they make a large impact. Unless the citizen is willing to take such responsibilities, the nation may sink into new quagmires beyond Vietnam. Or the United States may drift into an isolation that has proved to be disastrous for the national welfare.

In a more positive vein, there has developed since the end of World War II a new form of diplomacy known as citizen diplomacy. Where the old-fashioned diplomacy was limited to contacts between governments, the newer citizen diplomacy envisions nearly unlimited contacts between Americans and citizens of all nations. It is a quiet and unspectacular diplomacy but it has the potential, over the long run, for bringing about a more peaceful, or at least a less hostile, world. Citizen diplomacy is based on the simple but hopeful idea that if an American and someone in another land get to know one another, they are less likely to want to start shooting at each other. The Russian who is a convinced Marxist visiting an American home will not change his mind about the evils of capitalism and the inevitability of its collapse. But knowing a farmer in Iowa, or a steelworker in Pittsburgh, or a teacher in Denver will probably lessen his sense of threat from the United States. Similarly, the American who is a convinced capitalist will not become a convert to Communism if he visits a Russian home. But he will see the Russian and his family as human beings with problems much like his own and not as a potential target for bombs. Advocates of citizen diplomacy argue that getting university students involved is particularly important. From their ranks will come most of the future leaders of their nations. If they have met and formed friendships with their contemporaries in other lands during their formative years, they may be more receptive to reason and negotiation than to emotion and shooting when they arrive in positions of national responsibility.

Beyond the lessening of hostile feelings, those who have engaged in citizen diplomacy may find constructive ways to work out political, economic, and social problems that affect large portions of the human race, no matter where they live. The way in which pollution is attacked in Pittsburgh may be instructive to people living in the Ruhr Valley. The prevention of crime in Tokyo may be applicable to bringing down the crime rate in New York. It is an ancient idea, but still a useful one, that there are always things to be learned from other people.

In 1970, a young business executive, Alan A. Reich, was brought into the State Department as a Deputy Assistant Secretary for Educational and Cultural Affairs. He was particularly charged with stimulating more citizen diplomacy. As a student some years earlier, he had taken part in an exchange program in Yugoslavia and had found it rewarding, not the least of which was being introduced aboard ship on the way over to the young lady who later became his wife. In the spring of 1970, Mr. Reich told an audience in Coral Gables, Florida, that there were "100,000 volunteers throughout the United States who provide home hospitality to international visitors, academic exchanges involving close to a quarter million students and professors annually, tours abroad by artistic and sports groups, thousands of professional exchanges and hundreds of international conferences, tailored observation trips to the United States for thousands of influential international visitors annually, numerous private visits to the United States by multinational groups, exchanges of thousands of teen-age youth and members of such organizations as the Chambers of Commerce, 4-H Clubs of America, YMCA, Rotary, Lions, Kiwanis, and many exchanges resulting from the 350 sister-city affiliations with cities of other countries and hundreds of university to university affiliations.

109

"These are but a few of the many ways," Mr. Reich continued, "in which private Americans are in direct, open communication with peoples of other countries. They are important to all of us and to the American people in improving our international relationships, lessening the likelihood of hostility resulting from misunderstanding, and reinforcing tendencies to constructive cooperation by governments and peoples. Government decisions are based increasingly on the opinions and feelings of peoples, and false, stereotyped and simplistic views must be minimized through greater people-to-people understanding.

"The revolution in communications and transportation," he went on, "has brought peoples into direct, open, and immediate contact, making diplomacy a public matter. International diplomacy is no longer the business solely of the foreign offices of the world. This people-to-people communication has become a dominant force in international relations. Foreign offices can no longer confine themselves to speaking with other foreign offices for peoples; they are helping and encouraging peoples to speak for themselves across national boundaries."

Mr. Reich quoted Representative Dante B. Fascell, who represented his Florida audience in the Congress. Mr. Fascell had said earlier: "Today the success or failure of foreign policy undertakings may be affected more profoundly by what particular groups of people think and say than by the workings of traditional diplomacy."

Index

111

Index

Index

National Security Agency (NSA), 52, 54–55

National Security Council (NCS), 4, 12–18, 19, 21, 23, 25, 28, 39, 40, 41, 43, 44, 52, 63, 97; Ad Hoc Groups, 16–17; Defense Program Review Group, 17; Interdepartmental Groups, 16, 28, 39; Senior Review Group, 16, 20; Undersecretaries Committee, 18, 21; Washington Special Action Group, 17–18, 43, 44

National Security Decision Memorandum (NSDM), 21

National Security Study Memorandum (NSSM), 19

Nehmer, Stanley, Deputy Assistant Secretary of Commerce, 64

Nationalist China, lobby for, 94, 95

Neilan, Edwin P., 66

New York Times, 8

Nixon, President Richard M., 6, 15, 16, 18, 19, 21, 25, 38, 39, 41, 42–45, 59, 61, 62, 63, 64, 65, 73, 75, 79, 80, 90, 92, 97–98, 104

Nixon Administration, 61, 76, 78, 97, 107

Nixon Doctrine, 38

North Atlantic Treaty Organization (NATO), 37

Northwest Orient Air Lines, 92

Office of Emergency Preparedness, Director, 12

Office of Management and Budget, 89; Director, 17

Okinawa, return to Japan, 18–22, 79, 80

On War (von Clausewitz), 35

Operation Intercept, 68

Pan American Airways, 92

Park Chung Hee, 86

Peace Corps, 26

Pentagon Papers, 8, 36

Peterson, Peter, 65

Petty, John R., 60

Philadelphia Council of World Affairs, 99

Post Office, 63

Powers, Francis Gary, 49

Present at the Creation (Acheson), 12

President of the United States, 4, 5, 11–22, 55, 74, 105, 107

President's Council of Economic Advisers, Chairman, 17

President's Science Adviser, 17

Public Law 480, 62

Pueblo, U.S.S., intelligence ship, 49, 86

RAND Corporation, 96

Reich, Alan A., 109–110

Reichauer, Edwin O., 97

Richardson, Elliot L., 18

Rogers, William P., 15, 19, 21, 25, 26, 39, 43, 44, 64, 73, 76

Rooney, Representative John J., 66

Roosevelt, President Franklin D., 11, 49, 72

Rostow, Walt W., 14, 97

Rush, Michael M., 89, 90

Rusk, Dean, 14, 25, 26, 39, 100

Sato, Eisaku, 22, 64, 79

Secretary of Defense, 12, 38, 39, 55

Secretary of State, 9, 12, 21, 24, 28, 32, 38, 39, 55, 59

Securities and Exchange Commission (SEC), 89, 90

Senate, 79: Appropriations Committee, 77; Armed Services Committee, 40, 77; Commerce Committee, 77; Foreign Relations Committee, 71, 73, 77, 78, 79, 80

Shannon, Thomas F., 96

Sihanouk, Prince Norodam, 42

Smallwood, H. K., 85–88

Sorge, Richard, 49

Sorensen, Theodore, 13

South Africa, U.S. policy toward, 6

Southeast Asia Treaty Organization, 37

Soviet Union, 36, 100

Stans, Maurice H., 64

Status of Forces Agreements (SOFAs), 84, 85, 87, 88

Supreme Court of the United States, 84, 87

Symington, Senator Stuart, 76, 78

Texas Border Patrol, 69

Thurmond, Senator Strom, 63

Tonkin Gulf Resolution of 1964, 72, 79

Index

Transpacific air route controversy of 1968–1969, 90–91

Truman, President Harry S, 12, 25, 39, 72

Turkey, and opium production, 68

U-2 flights, 49, 51

Undersecretary of State, 17, 28

Undersecretary of State for Political Affairs, 18, 28

United Nations, 65, 67

United Nations Food and Agricultural Organization, 62

United States Chamber of Commerce, 66

United States Coast Guard, 69

United States Court of Appeals, 84, 86

United States Information Agency (USIA), 19, 23, 26

United States-Japan Trade Council, 95

United States Universal Code of Military Justice, 84

Ushiba, Nobuhiko, 65

Versailles Peace Treaty, 72

Vice President of the United States, 12

Vietnam, 14, 26, 36, 38, 39, 72, 77, 103, 104, 106–107

von Clausewitz, General Karl Maria, 35

Washington, President George, 3

Westinghouse Electric Corporation, 67, 68

Wheeler, General Earle G., 43, 44

Whiting, Allen, 97

Wilson, Charles, 39

Wilson, President Woodrow, 72